An Odyssey
in Blue

Also by Joseph M Labaki

Inconscient Et Sexualite

A Riffian's Tune

An Odyssey in Blue

An autobiographical novel

JOSEPH M LABAKI

CLUNETT PRESS

Published by Clunett Press, UK, 2018

First published in Great Britain in 2018

ISBN: 978-0-9926484-3-5

All names of the individuals in this book are fictitious
but the story is based on reality

ACKNOWLEDGEMENTS

I would like to thank the friends and colleagues without whom this work would not have been possible:

To Stuart Polson, who managed, once again, to convey my book into one beautiful image.

To Stephen Raw, for making *An Odyssey in Blue* be spectacular in its own right.

To Alexandra, for taking on some of my responsibilities and giving me the gift of time.

To my editor Katherine Trail, for allowing me to keep my voice and give a platform to Jusef's.

To Maryam, for her continued encouragement and love.

To Ruth, for her readiness to lend a listening ear and extend a hand of help.

To my wife Sherry, who once again intertwined her life with Jusef's; thank you for being the loving light that guides my dreams home. I am blessed.

To all of you, my deepest appreciation.

For Sherry, Maryam and Ruth

GLOSSARY

Aalwi:	a small tribal village in Kebdana
abaya:	a simple, loose over-garment, essentially a robe-like dress
babouche:	leather slippers with no heel and very pointed toes
Fatiha:	that which opens a subject or a book or any other thing
Fezzy hat:	a tall, round hat with a tassel hanging from the top
hafiz:	one who knows the Koran by rote
jellabah:	a long, loose garment with a hood and long sleeves
jinn:	in Islamic mythology, any of a class of spirits, lower than the angels, capable of appearing in human and animal forms and influencing humankind for either good or evil
koffars:	the deniers of Allah and His unity
muezzin:	the person appointed at a mosque to lead, and recite, the call to prayer at every event of prayer and worship in the mosque.

Oulad Monhand:	a tribe; *oulad* means sons (of Monhand)
shari'a:	law, seen as deriving from the Koran
souk:	traditional bazaar market
Tarifit:	unwritten language of the Rif region of Morocco
thboyout:	a small bread roll
ʒawiya:	an Islamic religious school or monastery

I

With an insatiable hunger for education and loathing for a life soaked in harsh poverty, I travelled from the north of Morocco, the tribe of Kebdana — *Aalwi* — to the Moroccan capital in the south. Knocking at every office, seeking a grant for the university, I slept rough on the beach and lived on bread and water for weeks.

Perched on the Atlantic Ocean, Rabat struck me as a beautiful bird, but with two contradicting wings and so many contrasts. I wondered how this bird was able to fly and land on its feet. *A whirling dynamism is at work stealthily*, I thought. The French, well-housed, well-fed, well-dressed and well-educated, lived in the new town in big houses with large windows, decorated doors, gardens peppered with oranges and lemons at the front and back and a plethora of local servants. In hurtful contrast, the indigenous people lived like moles in the old town in narrow streets, with no windows, and were constantly struggling to emulate a language which was not theirs and imitate a way of life into which they were not born. The contrast hurt.

I saw no French buying or reading a Moroccan newspaper in Arabic. No French ever joined us in the mosque, though, naively, I expected this. No Moroccan worshipped in the daylight with *koffars* (the deniers of Allah and His unity). As the city was divided into old and new, it was also divided into poor and rich, Muslim and Christian, socialists and go-getters.

Under the siege of French culture and language, the new town was packed with embassies, diplomats, secret police, propagandists . . . Hence, the cost of living was kite-high. I had come here to seek a grant and had failed.

*   *   *

STOMACH FLIPPED, NERVES BROKEN, I made a U-turn. I boarded a juggernaut, a night coach, and headed home to the north, the Rif, renowned for hashish trafficking and its rugged mountains with people to match. Travelling in the night was both romantic and spooky. The signposts sometimes looked like real people and sometimes like *jinn*. With pent-up anger, I pondered what to do. *Pray*, I told myself. *If all power is in the hand of God, politics is certainly in the hand of man.*

Dawn crept through the windows, and the conductor turned on his radio. It wasn't Moroccan music we heard. It was Egyptian. *Another alienation. Do we not have good musicians? Or good singers? What's happened to our own music?*

Alighting from the coach in Nador and a few metres away from the station, I fell upon Uncle Mimoun. A fezzy hat covering his forehead, he looked smart and cheery in a dark brown suit with a creamy shirt underneath. Something was different, however, as his grey hair stood like a lamppost covering his ears. I recalled the horror and the feeling the grey colour triggered in him.

'I want to be immortal, an axolotl, young forever,' he had

once told us over the dinner table while we had sat cross-legged around it.

Realising I was tired, he shuffled me to a café in the middle of a plaza. We sat under a palm tree and, facing the sea with its stench of raw sewage, ordered two doughnuts and mint tea.

Scoffing his doughnut and sipping his tea, he asked me, 'Have you succeeded? Got a grant?'

'No,' I answered.

Silence.

'Give up,' he advised me. 'How is Rabat?'

'It's the centre of good and evil,' I replied.

'Safe?' he asked.

'Provided you trust no one and believe no one.'

'It's time for me to repent. I would like you to go with me to the *zawiya* soon. I feel spiritually dry. But I am nervous and don't know what to expect. My wife Mimount is against it, and intense hesitation is twirling in my mind,' he said.

'Sorry. I'm going to resume currency trading in the black market; they're worlds apart. I have nothing to live on,' I answered. 'You must know that.'

Finished sipping our tea, we parted ways. Buttoned-up with anger and frustration, I headed to Mr Amakran. On my way, I reminded myself of the force I was about to face. He was rich and shrewd, could be both mean and generous. He could be as hot as fire or as cold as a fish. Though he loved women and wine, he was always wise. Like the Atlantic's waves, his business was always on the move, from rich to richer.

A stroke of luck! When I arrived at his cash and carry, I found him sitting in his armchair just like an old king, a silver tray with a silver teapot and gold-rimmed glasses in front of him. His son Soad was sitting beside him and counting a pile of cash reaching his chin. From a distance, they looked big and comfortable.

Feeling like an intruder, having nothing to sell or to buy, I saluted them. Mr Amakran lifted his head, put his glasses on and peered at me as though he had never seen me. My appearance suddenly jogged his memory; a smile stretched his beard.

'Come! Good to see you!' he called to me in his tenor voice. 'I wondered what had happened to you! Your Uncle Mimoun has been out of sight for a while. How is he?'

'He's here in the town. He's the same. A rifle on his shoulder and scouring the sky for prey.'

Mr Amakran's son perplexed me. I had never met him or known anything about him. Mr Amakran didn't talk about his family. Soad looked to be in his mid-thirties, quiet and polite. Breaking my spell, Mr Amakran blurted out, 'Soad is going to get married soon. Would you like to be his best man?'

This is a farce, I thought to myself. Then, my mind bolted. *Is this Soad's first marriage? The sons of wealthy men don't get married late, and rarely just once.* I felt my mind was running away with me like a wild horse.

'I would like to borrow some money from you, Mr Amakran,' I said.

Soad immediately glared at me.

'No grant?' asked Mr Amakran.

'No,' I answered.

'You should know the currency market has changed. It's now run by gangs, syndicates, mafia, you name it. Banks are no longer empty shells. They've beefed up their coffers. In fact, they compete with the black market themselves.'

Listening to Mr Amakran, I felt a chill. 'Could you lend me three thousand dirhams?' I asked.

'No.'

I felt ice covering my toes. He paused, stood up and sat down again. My mind twirled; no grant and no loan. Mr Amakran stretched out his hand and yanked out a shabby case from below his thighs. It was bulging with cash in different currencies, counted and tied.

With no fuss or paper to sign, he handed me three thousand dirhams. 'No interest. Just my money back,' he said.

Thrilled, I shook his hand and left. I serpentined to the open *souk*, a square yard, walled all around and with one single main entrance door, a throwback to its Spanish heritage. Armed police, batons dangling on their left sides, a rifle for long distance on their backs, sat outside the door to collect the entry taxes. Regional farmers flocked to sell their goods; they stood side by side with fishermen, butchers, second-hand sellers and sardine fryers. The *souk* was choked with cafés, doughnut-bakers and local doctors offering blood-sucking creatures to reduce blood pressure and lighten the head. People came here to shop, drink, gamble, play dominos, preach to each other and share and spread ignorance. In the *souk*, one could buy or sell, gamble or smoke, do everything except make love or talk politics. People melted into one single flesh, a blanket of joy and smiles.

When I entered the *souk*, I felt human flesh, I palpated its pulse, but I also reminded myself of its traps. I searched for a weapon to protect Mr Amakran's money and fell in love with a knife, a switchblade, shiny, beautiful and frightening.

Still morning and wrapped in hopes, I boarded a cramped coach, wove myself into the crowd of men, women and children, and headed to the border between two zebras: Melilla in Spain and Morocco, between Europe and Africa. Past midday, out of the coach at the border, fear and anxiety struck me. My mind pedalled into infinite possibilities. *What if my money is confiscated? How would I pay it back?* This scenario swirled intensely in my mind.

Seized by *angoisse* and still in Morocco, I barricaded myself in a café and filled my stomach with overly sweet espresso until it clenched and ended in a knot. I watched men, old and young, women, tall and beautiful, like ants with no scouts, looking and scavenging for something. *A busy life? No. They're haunted. It's a move. It's a push. It's a race. It's simply chaos.*

Sitting there with only my thoughts, and watching the women and families, I was reminded of Khadija. I wondered what was going on in her life. I wrote a poem and a long, romantic letter to her, hoping to see her soon. Glued to my chair, my body gained weight and felt heavy, but my mind flew wild, which wasn't a help.

I spied a man eyeing me. From time to time, the sun beamed into the room, glared on the floor and washed him. He hid behind sunglasses. I was sure he was watching me; I kept glancing at him and scribbled how many beers and glasses of wine he downed. He struck me as a foreigner, neither Moroccan nor Spanish, a *bastard*, as we called them in school. I convinced myself that he was a CIA agent – *black angel*, we had nicknamed them. You can't see them, but they can see you. When in doubt, they kill you.

With clouds in the sky matching my mind, I left the café when I saw a cortege on its way to Melilla. Someone important, certainly a diplomat, was going to cross. I watched the border police, both Spanish and Moroccan, lift the barriers. As the cortege got closer, I realised it was a funeral procession. A Spanish consul had died in Nador, I learned later, and a huge hearse was followed by many cars with pedestrians on both sides of the road. The conundrum I couldn't fathom was how so many Moroccan women could be crying for a foreigner they didn't know or love.

As a Spaniard, he can only be a koffar, I thought. *Peat for hell.* Then I remembered my father had told me that in death, even a man's penis was holy. But death, it was said, was an octopus. If it missed you, it would take one of your loved ones. It would let you cry alone and struggle on your own.

I felt light and joined the mourners. I pushed through and laid my hand on the hearse. I wasn't genuine, but I wasn't detached either. Slowly and with huge dignity, the cortege crossed the border. I found myself suddenly in Spain with three thousand dirhams in my pockets.

I boarded the red city bus and headed to the Melilla plaza. Still leery of what Mr Marjosi had done to me, I avoided Café Morina, my haven. For a few pesetas, he and his ring had tried to slay me in a most holy place: the cathedral. In revenge, pride and utter stupidity, I had bought a pistol and cornered him. By the grace of God, I hadn't killed him and hadn't become a murderer. I would have been a criminal, just like him.

In fear and caution, I chose a café a distance away but still on the elegant main boulevard crowded with chic shops. Sitting on a chair behind a high table, I watched plump Spanish women hustle up and down the street. I wished I could communicate with them, but could only offer silence and isolation. Searching for differences and similarities between the Spanish and me, I concluded, *I am not one of them. My social DNA is 99.97% different.*

Under the cloak of night, the ship docked around nine. No sooner had it anchored than the crowd poured out, but an even bigger throng was waiting. The travellers, mainly Moroccan, were received with kisses and hugs. No one was timid or embarrassed. I saw a lava of emotion, the tears trickling down, and the joy of reunion.

I started trading and shouted, 'Exchange! Deutschmarks, dollars, French francs!' No clients. Batting around, I shouted louder, offered a cracking rate, higher than my competitors. A flock of men heeded my words, stopped, crowded me, and we began bargaining, my hand never far away from my knife.

As I was in the midst of exchanging currency, a burly man crept from behind and put his hand over my mouth. He was big, prepared, determined and trained. Choking, I swung my neck right and left. Alas, he completely overpowered me. I hoped for intervention from my client or the crowd, but, unconcerned, no one bothered. Like worms, the crowd squirmed away.

Using every muscle I possessed, I somehow managed to dislodge his hand and give him an elbow punch in the chest. 'You're in private territory,' he hissed deep into my ears. 'You aren't a member of the syndicate, little scab. You haven't paid your dues.'

'True,' I told him, hoping he would let me go and pay later.

He spread his fingers and dove at my eyes to blind me. I dodged. Using both his right and left hand, he showered me with heavy punches. I reeled with dizziness.

Swerving, I shouted, 'My brother will kill you!' In fact, I had no brother, but I wished I had. I yanked out my knife. As my switchblade sparkled in the starry night, I grazed his shoulder.

He backed away and ordered me, 'Never put your foot on my turf!'

I abandoned trading on the dock and headed to the taxi station, which was more heavily policed. 'Boy!' a man standing on his own called to me. I ignored him, for I didn't like the word.

Two men waiting for a taxi, looking lost, shouted across, 'Do you know where to get dirhams?'

'I'm a trader,' I shouted back.

The two men had just arrived from Holland and had worked in Heerlen in the mining industry. They spoke no Spanish or Arabic, just broken patois. They bought all my dirhams. I made a fortune.

To sleep and feel safe, I searched for a hotel and strolled slowly to the top of the street known as a melting pot for mixed races. A cluster of hotels, most of them brothels, all bathed in flashing lights, were dazzling pedestrians and philanderers. I picked the best of a bad lot. Once inside the hotel, I felt Mr Amakran's money was safe.

At the front desk was a Spanish woman, looking beautiful with large, dancing hips. 'I'm the owner,' she told me.

I was sure she didn't like my looks; she could tell I'd been bruised and fighting. As well as the madam, she was also a prostitute, busy trading for her own account. I paid for my room and she tossed me the key. Climbing the stairs, glancing back, I caught her sneering at me. I squared my shoulders and walked on. I'd fought enough that evening.

My room was tiny, and the bed, looking like a bunk, was resting on very tall metal legs. Lying in it, I felt like a chicken in a coop. A dirty grey sheet, left untucked, dangled over the mattress, and two pillows, over-filled and hard, were dotted with human hair, some long, some short, some dark, some blonde. It was obvious the bed had been ridden hard, but for me, the room was heaven and a haven.

Hunger pangs forced me out and into the night to search for a bakery with some food to take away. I came upon the entire lobby filled with women, old and young. Some struck me like lost kids. All looking subdued, some on a chair, others on a sofa rubbing shoulders, they watched fearfully for whoever was moving, coming and going. A herd of middle-aged men were leaning against the wall and gazing at them. Some were drinking, some smoking and some both, peering at the girls and picking their prey. Some poorly dressed men looked like feral dogs and girls, like starved rabbits. Whenever a deal was struck, the man paid the boss and trailed behind the woman, both disappearing somewhere into the bowels of the hotel. The madam was a strict timekeeper.

Outside the hotel, I heard a cacophony of languages; some

I understood, but most escaped me. I bought a Spanish baguette, called *thboyout* in Berber , and a tin of sardines. Afraid of the snooping woman's strict rules, I scoffed it in the street.

Drowned in sleep in bed, I was awakened by the thundering voice of an outraged man. A chorus of shouts ensued. Feigning deafness, I stayed in bed, my head plunged into the pillow. The yelling didn't fade, and sleep deserted me. Curious, I stepped out of the room, peered over the railing and ventured into the lobby.

There was a man, cuffed, his hands behind his back, wrestling with himself, and two armed police standing on each side. The man was a volcanic potty mouth, insulting everything and everybody, sparing no religion. The manageress looked well-rehearsed for this scene, calm, poised, and was moving around with provocative hips, right and left, up and down, exciting even the dead. *This scene must be familiar to her*, I thought as I returned to my room.

The large hotel had only one toilet on each floor. As dawn broke, the queues grew long and intimidating. A Spanish woman, meaty and heavy-boned with short legs and fat thighs, in pyjamas open and hanging, waited while leaning against the wall. She wasn't shy and reminded me of my provincial tribe where women had to travel one kilometre to hide, pee and wipe themselves with stones.

As sunlight beamed into the room, I descended the stairs. Reaching the lobby, I found three women mopping the beautifully tiled floor. A mountain of bottles of wine of all sizes had been drunk. The mixed smell made the lobby seem like a factory. A creek of blood, and not far away, another puddle, reminded me of the remnants of a downpour. It was still too fresh for the flies and mosquitoes to discover.

'What happened?' I whispered to a woman cleaner, who looked undisturbed.

'Just a tiff,' she replied with an ironic voice and smile. She nodded and leaned toward me. 'Men and women come here for lust. Some buy and some sell; no difference between here and the grocery market. Sadly, however, some expect loyalty, faithfulness, commitment: qualities hard to find even in one's own home, let alone here, my son.'

Leaving her behind, I mulled over her words and sauntered to a bohemian café. The morning was bright with only a few fluffy clouds roaming the sky. The café was packed; continental breakfasts, light and tasty, attracted loud and lively men and women, but they all looked filthy. Trousers filled with holes were long and swept the floor. Unattractive shoes looked like soldiers' boots, jackets were wrinkled and old, and shirts were unbuttoned. I wondered how they were able to pay for their breakfasts.

Puffed with cash, like wadded newsprint, that no one wanted to buy, I took a coach to the border. A man on a scooter shouted, 'Ride to Nador!' We bargained and finally agreed a price. I made sure he knew I carried a knife. Only God knew what he himself carried. We needed, but mistrusted, each other and both expected the worst. He drove his scooter, and I sat behind him, digging solidly into his hips. It was an uncomfortable position for me. Flying, not one single word was uttered.

'Where in Nador do you want to be dropped?' he finally asked me.

'*Parada.*'

'No,' he said.

I presumed he was avoiding either the police or a gang. He dropped me at the entry to the town, miles away from the *parada*.

I paid him, we shook hands and parted.

2

From the centre of the town, I walked until I reached the prison. Standing at the gate, I pondered. *Why did she kill Mrs Malani? There are so many closets to this murder. Was there a man involved? Was there a third party? Was it emotional, lust, vengeance, financial, or simple madness? Because I will never know, my feeling is free. Love or hate. I love her. She was my sister; she was a mule, a bucking bronco who never faltered. She has a child whose father loves only bingo, cigarettes, siestas and wine.*

My mind racing and my emotions feeling like a violin string wound too tight, I entered the prison gate. Filling the form, showing my ID, I went in search of Rabbia. The prison ground was unkempt and looked like it belonged to an asylum; rubbish bins dotted the corners and litter flew in the breeze. Like marionettes or ghosts, the prisoners were moving slowly, resigned to their days with no tomorrows.

'Can you call Rabbia?' I asked a passing warden. She swiftly glared at me and craned her neck, sweeping the sky as if expecting Rabbia to be on a rooftop.

Finally, she responded. 'Wait here.' She motioned with her finger, giving me the impression I shouldn't be there.

I waited for one hour and yet there was no sign of Rabbia. *Is she here?* Then, a woman emerged out of the blue, looking disoriented and hobbling slowly. *It's not Rabbia,* I convinced myself, for this woman looked shabby, shrivelled, wrinkled and with no shred of life in her.

Moving in my direction like a spectre, she yelled and shuffled toward me. Her looks and gestures spooked me. Without a word, I found myself sandwiched between her arms.

'Are you still my brother?' she sobbed.

Unable to hold back my tears, I joined her. I expected her to talk about her son, as mothers do. She didn't. *Has she already forgotten him?* We didn't converse. No topic was appropriate; words were hard to find.

'What can I do for you?' I asked with a choked-up throat. Looking at her, I thought of food and clothes.

'Take me out of here,' she begged.

'So many hurdles!' I replied, knowing that wasn't what she wanted to hear.

I left Rabbia with no hope, knowing that neither she nor I could afford a lawyer's fees. She was emotionally distraught, and I was rattled when we parted. Leaving the prison, I walked along the railway to the town centre. On impulse, feeling the money heavy with hope in my pocket, I searched for a lawyer.

Mr Ash was a divorce and criminal lawyer. Whoever could afford him and reached him first won the case. It was rumoured he could divorce a couple while they were on their honeymoon, dispossess one of his house while he was mortgage-free and the title under his pillow. Not only was he a master of the written law, but his interpretation of it amounted to a new law. Those behind the desk in the court winked when they saw him in his robe. He had a name in the town and was a giant in the court.

Coming across his office, I knew how lucky I was. It was impressive with two wide glass windows, his picture hanging in each, a symbol that no matter where you went in Nador, there was no one much better than he. He was widely portrayed as friendly and approachable. Staring at his portrait, I succumbed to what I had heard: nothing in his hand could go wrong. Sheepishly, I stepped into his office.

The reception was wide, sea- and sun-facing, decorated with two beautiful, well-dressed local girls, both with black hair, sharp eyes, aristocratic noses and innocent smiles. I received attention I had never had or deserved. His secretary, Layla, took me to his office and introduced me. He stood up, and I was received with dignity and style. Far from his desk, in a small corner, we sat at a bare table with a lazy Susan in the middle. His office looked like a public library with books shining behind the glass and files covering one entire wall. That was how I had imagined a Parisian lawyer after reading book after book, but I was in Nador, provincial Africa. *This is a social aberration*, I thought.

'What do you do?' he asked.

'I'm a trader and student,' I said.

A twirling thought scribbled on his face. 'What has brought you here?' he asked.

'My sister Rabbia was convicted of murdering Mrs Malani, a herbalist.'

He paused, stood up and pulled a file from his cabinet. With sadness washing over his face, he said, 'I know the case. I was the ad hoc prosecutor. Your next step would be to launch an appeal, but I am excluded.'

His rhetoric and oratory possessed me. I admired it.

He pulled one book by Karl Marx and booklets by Lenin and the Bolsheviks from the shelf and handed them to me. Thirsty for reading material, I grabbed the gift, acknowledged his generosity, but didn't yet know that I left carrying grenades.

Tired and bruised, I left the town and headed toward Makran and Tassamat, home, seeking a peaceful life with no pollution, no cars, no threats, no noise except the cries of foxes and hoots of owls, an orchestra for a lonely, ghostly night.

In my family's stone farmhouse with two bedrooms and a barn, on a hill peeking over the Mediterranean Sea, I cocooned myself for days. My life fell into a sinkhole. The sun lost its beam. The beauty around, hills, trees, lost their attraction. I pondered where my shepherding days had gone. This was a past I had lived, still lived, yet like my shadow, it kept me bound to the place, rooting me in it so I could never really escape. I decided to trade again.

While crossing the border into Melilla, a policeman spotted the books and took me in for an identity check. He looked evil from the start. He was tall with olive skin, wore a black suit, smoked a cigarette, his hand and lips shaky. He was certainly a ruthless man. After a lengthy interrogation, he became convinced I must be held in custody. In vain, I tried to explain myself and protested vigorously.

'Wait, wait,' was all I got.

At twilight, a man and woman jumped out of a white car. They looked the epitome of sophistication, slim and attractive with black suits and sunglasses, like they belonged in another world. They swished past me and grabbed my books from a small table. They browsed and twittered. The small room was just big enough to hold three of us, and I sat sandwiched between them, feeling trapped in a crocodile's jaws.

'What is the purpose of these books?' the man asked.

'To read them,' I answered.

'Do you need to carry them all with you to read?'

'No,' I said.

'What do you do?' he asked.

'Currently, I am trading currency . . . in the hope to finance my studies,' I added.

'Bastard!' the woman shouted. 'How did those books fall into your hands?'

'A lawyer gave them to me,' I answered. I should have known lawyers were not popular.

'Are you on a mission?' she asked cynically, grinning.

'Mission?' I asked.

'Communism,' she answered. Annoyed, she stood up, lit a cigarette, kicked the floor like a *toro*, then, with her right hand full of jewellery, poked me in the face. Unrelenting, she sat down and lit another cigarette, then came to me with a smack, bringing lightning to my eyes.

Women don't do that, I thought. *They are soft, hands and heart, but not this one*. I stood up and shouted, 'No!' Her colleague pushed me back down into the chair.

'Is anyone expecting to receive those books from you?' the man asked, pretending innocence.

'No,' I said.

'Simply a trader?' he asked.

'Definitely.'

'Your capital?'

I delved into my pocket and yanked out everything I had. Both quiet, they shrugged. To ward off any questions, I handed her the bank receipt, and that proved to be my saving grace. Meanwhile, the man browsed through the books.

'The books belong to Mr Ash!' he shouted, pointing to the stamp inside the front cover.

'Yes!' I butted in. 'I have them on loan.'

They left the room, and I was alone to guess and wonder. I peeked outside the room; few police were on duty. I took a risk and sneaked out.

Carefully, I sauntered out of the station. Flagging down a passing taxi, I left hell behind. As if my brain were in my feet, I found myself in Mr Amakran's big shop. Happy and relaxed, he was on the phone with a Spanish woman. Nothing was innocent. I could hear her giggling. Seeing him busy and happy, I laid his money on his table. As I left his shop, I decided to do no more currency trading. I'd had enough.

3

As I was not trading, Uncle Mimoun hired me to help him and his wife Mimount on Soad's wedding day. What an opportunity to make some money, see people and feast! I left home, crossed the creek and joined Uncle Mimoun and his wife. Mimount was vainly beautifying herself as if it were her own wedding. She wore new clothes and had tried to braid her hair extensions in an eccentric way to look young and attractive. Watching her, I wondered if she had someone in mind other than Uncle Mimoun, a doubt I had never had before.

In contrast, Uncle Mimoun was less engaged and pretty unkempt. *Something is on his mind*, I thought. To make a public impression, he sent me to the town to hire a taxi. As a gift to Soad, he took a buck. Uncle Mimoun sat in the front beside the driver; his wife and I sandwiched the buck in the back seat. I tried to cuddle it, but it bleated all the way along. I tried everything to tame it, but it refused. It sensed its demise, and I felt sorry for it, but could do nothing. Nearing the house, we honked louder and louder like crazy in the hope Mr Amakran's neighbours would hear, come out to see us and notice our gift.

Mr Amakran's house was truly a palace, a complex sunk in a clump of trees: olives, figs, pomegranates and peaches.

Hugging it all was a thicket of huge prickly pear, peppered with aloe vera trees, the feeding ground for honey bees when winter bit with its ugly teeth and shut off its supply to its own frail, living creatures. A stone wall, two metres high, was built as support for the prickly pear.

With his two wives, Stee and Yamina, Mr Amakran emerged, looking happy, and a smile vibrated under his beard.

'Go and join Soad,' he told me, as if I were familiar with the house. Stee took the lead. Led by Yamina, Mimount was added to the huddle of loud women confined to the house. Uncle Mimoun was assigned to a tent full of riffraff hashish smokers and a few rich men.

I joined Soad and found him crowded by brothers and cousins. Mucking about, his brothers were playing with two pistols, one just the size of a palm and the other substantially longer and fatter. I wished I could have one. Most of the time, Soad was lying on his back with a rock-solid pillow on his chest.

'This is your day,' I said.

Stee brought us a tray of tea and sweet almonds. The boys told me she was Mr Amakran's first wife, but now out of action. She had no room of her own and slept wherever she could find space, but she acted like Jiminy Cricket, her eyes on everybody. She constantly worked on Soad, making him chic, perfumed and unrecognisable. He changed his clothes every hour, but every time was the same: white collarless shirt, *abaya*, generous trousers and yellow *babouche* slippers. Soad looked like a star among us. *What a caring woman, and he is not even her own son*, I thought.

All day long, Soad's mother, Yamina, looked preoccupied. She checked on me, and I wondered why. I assumed Auntie Mimount had mentioned me to her. She came to Soad's room with a plate full of meat and sat in the midst of us. I feasted on it.

As she moved around, I realised how tall and thin she was, with fair skin, green eyes, golden hair and well-dressed for the occasion. She looked as if she were a kidnapped Swedish woman, out of place in the mountains of north Africa.

She took me aside, her eyes filled with anxiety, and said, 'Soad is under the spell of the local wizard, Mr Rihimy. He said that unless he were paid, he would ruin Soad, destroy his life, social reputation and marriage.'

'What can be done?' I asked.

'I want to thwart the threat and bribe the damn man.'

Yamina seems to have no confidante. Why has she waited until now?

'I'd like you to go with Stee,' she said.

'Yes, madam,' I replied.

Happy to leave Soad, his brothers and cousins, I accompanied Stee. Energetic, small and fat, in her mid-forties and adorned with tattoos on her forehead, chin, cheeks and neck, she lamented about her life all the way along as if we were old friends.

'Unappreciated,' she said. 'I am the doormat. Respect is what I want. Love is what I don't expect, and I didn't get it even when I was young, beautiful and attractive. Why should I get it now? I am not hungry, though, but neither is our dog. My parents sold me. Mr Amakran never paid me the full dot even though I was a virgin. He still owes me.'

I sighed with relief when we reached the wizard's house. His servant took us across the courtyard to the entrance of the wizard's salon.

Stepping inside, we took our shoes and socks off, then came face-to-face with Mr Rihimy. He was a handsome, heavy man with a long beard peppered with white, sitting arrogantly cross-legged on a mosaic rug and leaning against a tiled wall. On his right, stood a large, tall wooden box shaped like a pyramid. In the middle of it, a green candle flickered. He never lifted his gaze to watch us, but with eyes like a sheep's, peripherally alert, nothing escaped his feigned tiredness.

On his left side sat a stocky man, round face with a short beard, quiet and looking subdued. He eyed me with curiosity, and I reciprocated.

'He is from Saudi Arabia,' Mr Rihimy whispered.

Intrigued, I asked, 'Which town in Saudi Arabia are you from, sir?'

'Jeddah,' he replied politely.

A man from Saudi Arabia had heard about Mr Rihimy and travelled that far to come here? Mind boggling.

From the moment we sat down facing Mr Rihimy, Stee had been in a trance. She inched closer and closer to him to be blessed, but he never put his hand upon her.

On her order, I passed the money to Mr Rihimy. He opened his magic box, murmured a few words, picked some powder, dried leaves, small stones, handed them to Stee and said, 'Put that safely in the groom's room, under his pillow.'

Leaving Mr Rihimy, Stee looked ecstatic, but I was deeply sceptical. We returned to Mr Amakran's house and found it welling with high-spirited guests soaking in the celebratory atmosphere. Several tents were overflowing with men and the house was stretched beyond its walls with women. Soad confined himself to his room which was patrolled by his mother.

'Is Mr Rihimy satisfied?' she asked me.

'Seems so,' I replied as I handed her the packet with instructions.

* * *

THE NIGHT WAS WARM AND wind-free. With no clouds to hide their brilliance, the stars shone like cities in the sky. After the couscous, tagine and almond cake which Mr Amakran had provided with generosity, men left their tents and went out, handmade drums in hand. Disciplined dancers, they formed two opposing lines of over one hundred in each, moving back and forth in tandem.

As they moved erotically close to each other, they crossed obliquely and almost touched opposite cheeks and legs. There was nothing innocent in this dancing. It went on until dawn.

Women were also dancing behind the walls, out of sight and touch. Under the light of the carnival stars, I joined the crowd, singing and dancing.

Suddenly, I was hit by a thirst. My mouth became so dry that my tongue hurt. Soon after quenching my thirst, my visual field started to dissolve into an incoherent mosaic of colours. As I tried to stand up, my left hand and arm felt far heavier than my right. Hardly able to think or move, I took refuge in a small, shabby room full of old clothes and sheepskins.

I lost all sense of time and space. The room lost its geometric shape. Walls and their colours sank into unknown. They looked long with fuzzy colour; everything felt wobbly around me. Still lying on a rug, I closed my eyes to retrieve my sanity. I staggered to my feet, leaned against the wall and focused my eyes on the doorway, looking for an exit from madness. The hallway made with dried mud hit me like a long tarmac road. The door looked tall, but twisted and too narrow. Impassable. Panic. I lifted my head toward the ceiling; it struck me like a sky peppered with wafting fog. I looked right, left, up and down. A thick, heavy silence blocked my ears. My eyes, my ears, even my brain failed me.

Then it hit me: a tea brewed with home-grown hashish had been served.

* * *

WELL BEFORE DAWN BROKE, STEE awakened me. 'It's time to bring the bride home,' she told me.

As Soad's best man, I was also Mr Amakran's right hand. I sat beside him in his Mercedes. His two wives, Stee and Yamina, sat in the back.

Full of men, a column of cars, French, German, Italian, lined up and crept behind us. As if it were not his son's wedding day, Mr Amakran kept up his constant chatter about profit and loss. Sitting beside him, I had the task of listening. Tiny mirrors in their hands, his wives kept painting their cheeks, checking their faces and sprinkling their chests with perfume as if it were their own weddings.

'Can you lend me some money until next summer?' I asked him.

'To do what?' he asked.

'To go to the university,' I said. I was certain he would and hoped the joy of the day and the carnival atmosphere would soften his heart or cloud his mind.

'No,' he replied.

As if nothing had happened, I opened the window. The fresh air flooded the car and refreshed my face, but it didn't dig deep enough to wipe out my disappointment. Nearing the bride's house, our column of cars serpentined the road and filled the air with dust and honking horns. The bride's house was besieged. Old men and young boys were everywhere. Joy was in the air.

I opened the door to free Stee and Yamina. Clothed as brides themselves in long, traditional kaftans, they found it difficult to get out of the car. They strolled through the mob and went in to receive the bride. While Mr Amakran and I sat waiting in the car, the crowd, curious to see the bride, hovered around us.

Stee and Yamina took too long. Mr Amakran began to fidget. 'What's keeping them?' he asked me. 'People are waiting for us at home,' he added.

'The lamentation of separation might have taken too long,' I responded. 'It's a tear in the family; a living death.'

Guests in the cars behind us lost their patience and honked energetically. Then Stee emerged, like a cursed angel.

'There's no bride to come with us,' she said.

'Go back and wait!' Mr Amakran shouted in a panic.

In fear, she scurried inside again.

'Something isn't right,' I said to Mr Amakran.

Completely distraught, his wife Yamina came out.

Mr Amakran, despairingly, looked at me and said, 'Jusef, go in and see what has happened.'

I pushed through the crowd and found myself mixed with women I had never dreamed of seeing in my life: some beautiful and some you wouldn't look at twice. Getting distracted, I began to look for a wife for myself.

I asked for the bride's mother. Searching, I found her, jaw muttering and eyes welling, facing the wall.

'Mr Amakran is outside. We are here to pick up the bride, your daughter,' I told her. She neither responded nor even acknowledged my presence.

'Where is the bride, your daughter?' I asked her again. 'I am the groom's best man.'

'She was beautifully veiled, among us, happy and playful this morning. Suddenly, we couldn't find her. An angel snapped her away,' she wailed.

'Why are you here facing the wall?'

'I was praying she would be back before you came to pick her up. But . . .' she answered.

I realised how serious and chaotic it was. Heart pumping, I went to Mr Amakran. 'The bride bolted, and Soad has been jilted,' I told him.

He threw his hands and chest against the steering wheel. I could only see his skull. I heard a whirring anger in his chest. Frozen in time, I waited for him to straighten up. Finally, as if recovering from a coma, he opened his eyes and looked around, as if he were trying to figure out why he was there.

With no bride or pride, we set out for home, a trail of cars behind us. Driving, Mr Amakran uttered no words. I heard him breathing heavily and saw red flushes waving over his face.

Stee, behind us, started to talk, but he quickly shut her up. *For Mr Amakran, this is a curse from hell, but for her, revenge from heaven.*

Children had been bustling, jumping and dancing around the gate since dawn in anticipation of our return. They were excitedly expecting to be showered with sweets and peanuts by the bride. Mr Amakran's guests came out of their ornate tents and formed a half-moon around the gate. They hoped to get a glimpse of the new bride's face as she was carried to be received by her mother-in-law. Women inside the courtyard were standing on top of each other, excitedly waiting to see the bride smash an egg on the floor of her new room. As the yolk and white melded, magically the two families of in-laws would also be. So, too, would the cracked eggshell break any walls, be they of a social, jealous or competitive nature, between them.

Knowing the expectation, Mr Amakran avoided the main gate and detoured around the side of the house. He jumped out of the car, ducked through the side door and emerged through the front gate to face his guests.

'Dinner is served!' he yelled.

Standing beside him, I saw confusion on the faces of the guests. They stood for a minute, then dispersed toward the buffet tables.

I joined Soad in his room and found him shaved, drowned in perfume and preparing himself for the night when he would go to the bride's room and, for the first time, come face-to-face with the bride, waiting for him and surrounded by girls. He would be the sole male sitting beside the bride, with the girls serving them tea and nuts.

The girls would enjoy the sweet talk and dream while focusing on the couple. At midnight, they would leave the bride and groom alone. The erotic activity would commence and the result would be communicated: virginity or impotence. A flag, either white or red-stained, would be raised. But Soad would be denied this experience.

'Soad, the bride has vanished,' I told him, just as his father had instructed me to do.

'Is that a joke?' he retorted.

'The bride has bolted!' concurred Stee, who stood beside me.

Soad jumped up, his eyes frantic, his tongue desperately trying to moisturise his already dry lips. Tearing off his expensive bridal clothes, he stood naked, searched for old clothes and yelled, 'I will find her, catch her, kill her, bring her here . . .'

'She is not your wife yet,' I told him, trying to calm him.

'She's my wife! I have the deed!' he shouted. 'Signed, proved and endorsed by religious and legal authority. What is missing?'

'Consummation,' replied Stee.

'So, I have papers, but no wife!' he exploded.

'Until the penis's head has disappeared into the vagina, the marriage is not consummated,' explained Stee.

I was shocked to hear her. 'What type of knowledge you have!' I challenged her. 'I have been at school, I have my baccalaureate, I know Arabic and French, yet I have never heard that.'

'You were not taught the right things,' she said. 'This is shari'a. I was born with it and in it.'

Soad, now dressed in his old clothes, pushed Stee aside and left. We assumed he went to hunt for his bride. What he would do if he found her, we couldn't guess.

Searching for Mr Amakran, I found him with Yamina in a big room with the windows and the door closed. He was shivering like a shaman. His skin had changed in colour to pitch black and his eyes bugged out, oxblood red.

'It's about my honour, not about the bride,' he said and muttered again and again, 'My honour. My honour.'

Yamina was no help to him. She was self-destructing, peeling her skin off with her fingernails, blood dripping, and pulling out her hair. She was murmuring, too, and the word 'honour' was popping out again and again.

I felt deeply sorry for Mr Amakran, Soad and Yamina. He had been brought to his knees by Layla, the bride-to-be, whom he didn't even know.

Leaving Mr Amakran, I headed to find Uncle Mimoun. Like most male guests of his age, he didn't know what had happened. I found him lying against a tree and fiddling with his prayer beads. He was deeply relaxed, looking spiritually engaged. His eyelids quivered up and down like a baby chick hatching.

'This wedding is a fiasco!' I told him. 'The bride has bolted.' He looked at me as if I were telling a lie or, at best, mentally disturbed.

'Do you need to close your eyes while you are praying?' I asked him.

'Eyes are the gate of lust,' he answered. 'Go and tell Mr Amakran that I would like to talk to him.'

I knew Mr Amakran was in a state, but by now I had become familiar with the house and his family. I found him a bit calmer, but still outraged.

'What will people think?' he asked.

'Feed them. Let them dance and provide hashish for those who want it. You didn't worry about what your competitors in Nador thought or what poor people thought of you while passing and watching you in your luxurious chair, sipping tea and eating doughnuts dipped in honey. Uncle Mimoun wants to talk to you,' I said.

'Have you told him what happened?' he asked.

'Yes, I have.'

'Ask him to meet me at the end of the orchard near the river bank.'

By the time I saw Uncle Mimoun, he had already spoken with Mimount. 'I'm going to see Mr Amakran. Come with me,' he said to me. I felt a bit embarrassed as a boy walking with an old man through a wedding packed with young men. We waited for Mr Amakran for what seemed like hours. We all sat on stones as in biblical times.

'I have daughters, as you know. They've been brought up to know honour, to obey and respect the elderly and care for the sick. Some are already married. Blessed with girls, I have some still at home. The oldest is twelve. I would be happy to marry your son Soad to one of my daughters,' said Uncle Mimoun.

Mr Amakran's face lit up at Uncle Mimoun's offer. Between them, they concluded the marriage, but agreed the consummation would have to wait. Jamaa would move to Mr Amakran's house so she would learn, adapt to the family style and get familiar with Soad as husband and master.

On the same afternoon, two religious marriage officials arrived. Stee took them straight to a small, beautiful room overlooking the orchard. Charmingly, she brought tea and almond cake. Mr Amakran, Uncle Mimoun and I joined them. They looked respectable and full of humour.

'Who is getting married? Who is getting divorced? Who is marrying whom?' the old man asked. He turned to me. 'Are you the groom?'

Uncle Mimoun jumped in. 'My daughter Jamaa is marrying Mr Amakran's son Soad.' With a nod and hesitating voice, Mr Amakran blessed the union.

Before the two men left, we all recited the *Fatiha:*

> *In the name of God, the Lord of mercy and affection,*
> *The submission is to God, the Owner of the universe,*
> *The Merciful and the Forgiver, the Owner of the time.*
> *It's You that we worship and it's from You we seek help.*
> *Guide us on the straight path,*
> *The path of those You have chosen,*
> *And not the path of those You have rejected and who*
>   *have gone astray.*

The sun set and the night was grumpy. The sky was peppered with broken clouds, and the moon peeked through now and again. Overfed, the men dispersed into Mr Amakran's orchard and formed several exuberant choirs. Excited, some climbed the trees; others felt heavy and sat cross-legged below, forming a base.

The wedding festivities went on. Alas, there was no blood from the bride, no flag to fly or to cheer. Relatives who had come to see the precious blood would have to go back empty-eyed. It was, however, an occasion for men to discover how close they were to each other and listen to their flesh. The lid off, they danced with each other, drank and sang, with no guilt or feelings bottled. They discovered how intricately and intrinsically they were woven.

I was delighted that Mr Amakran had trusted me to be Soad's best man. He had introduced me to his home, which was like a fortress, but his trust didn't go as far as to give me a loan to start university. We were not wired to think alike. My hope was out of place and my time had ultimately been a loss.

*　　*　　*

DISAPPOINTED, I LEFT THE FOLLOWING morning with a guest of Mr Amakran, a lorry driver who traded in salt, spice and chicken. On our way to Melilla, we picked up another man. We all squashed into the front seat. The driver hardly put his hands on the steering wheel; they flew around theatrically. At the border, we passed through without being stopped or checked.

'Do they know you?' I asked the driver.

'No, they don't,' he said.

Then I suspected that salt, spice and chicken meant something else more costly and precious. Before reaching the centre, we came across a group of soldiers training. I was dropped at the centre to find my way.

I headed to Calle Acera de Reina Regente, the most dangerous and deprived street in the city, if not the world. Men and women of different races, religions and ages gathered here late in the afternoon, some to sell their clothes and home furnishings; others, simply curious, came to kill the boredom and be entertained by people brawling in the street. I arrived at two o'clock in the afternoon, not the best time. Shops, some selling melons, some selling shoes, some selling bread, were all closed for siesta and the street was unnervingly quiet.

Halfway up, I was accosted by two burly men. They suddenly stepped in front of me. There was no refuge anywhere on the street except in brothels, which were also closed.

Sandwiched between the two men, they cornered me against the wall. I noticed one of them was limping. *I am against one and a half,* I reassured myself, but as if compensating, the semi-disabled man was far more aggressive and stronger. He jabbed at my pockets, but my jacket was firmly buttoned. Veering and ducking was all I could do.

Resorting to my knife would have saved me, but would also have destroyed my dream and the reason I was there: to go to university. Wrapped in a cloud of fear, I lost the sense of space and time. Like a moon peeping out of a cloud, I spied a hotel on the left side of the street. It looked posh with a large door and baskets of flowers at the front. A vibrating voice gusted into my ears. *Run! Get in!*

I raced, and so they did, too. The gimpy man could not tag me, but his accomplice was only a few metres behind me. I could feel the heat of his breath on my neck as I flew into the hotel. They stopped abruptly at the entrance and looked like two wild dogs that had unexpectedly lost their prey. Despite the close call, I didn't regret coming to this godforsaken town and especially this street, for there had been no other choice.

The hotel lobby was wide and the entire floor was marbled with squares of white and black. Two sets of sofas were stuffed in a corner, facing a big, decorative double window. The hotel dwarfed the street. A bar covered the entire wall and was filled with hundreds of bottles of liquors. There were no chairs or tables in the bar, just high stools. I presumed Spanish people must enjoy their drinks, their talking and shouting while being uncomfortable and standing up.

In the middle of the hotel lobby was a short man behind a massive piano. He sounded like an amateur pianist, mixing staccato and legato notes in random fashion.

He stopped playing and shouted at me. 'What do you want?'

'One single bed,' I said. 'For two or three nights.'

'Pay now,' he said.

I didn't have easy access to my money. I moved to the corner, under his watch, and ripped open one pocket by pulling the thread. I shoved my hand in my pocket and yanked out some Spanish notes.

He didn't ask for my ID. He handed me the key and scurried back to his music. As I climbed the stairs, from nowhere, a thick, cloudy sadness suddenly washed over me. *Why do I feel like this? No lack of reasons: the society, its tradition, its religion, its politics and to top it all, I can't get a grant.*

The room was tiny and narrow. The paint was meant to last for generations, but it was dull, grey and too tired to last another day. A lamp dangled low, and I felt the heat whenever I stood up. In contrast, the bed seemed majestic, high and made out of steel, but the mattress was drooping down. It reminded me of a cow's udder in the spring season. There was no window except a small square at the top of the door to keep guests alive. Despite the conditions, I felt safe. As I lay on the bed, a forceful sleep grabbed me. I resisted, but lost.

At nine-thirty that evening, the bar downstairs was crowded and noisy. A swarm of voices made me wonder if there were any listeners among them. I heard a burst of laughter and envied those who were anxiety-free. I pulled the blanket over my head, trying to drown out their happiness.

At ten o'clock the following morning, people came out to face life and the street pulsed as usual. The street traders resumed their familiar bellows, and the crowd thickened and jostled. I climbed the hill and stood watching the collision of the two contradicting sisters: Europe and Africa. There was no war, but not much respect either.

It was on this spot where men and women came and sold their pants, rings, shoes, socks . . . Nothing there was worthless, except maybe people.

Standing, I faced a Spanish group of old men and women in black clothes, some with signs of bereavement, leaning against a wall and begging for money. Their voices, weak and cracking, emitted a sense of shame and humiliation.

Poverty and old age. What can be worse? I asked myself. I came upon a man selling new and used bras. Surrounded by women, he looked busy and popular. *This is the trade!* To test my theory, I bought twenty bras from him. Moving away, I stood in a corner, a high wall behind me, faced the throngs and shouted, 'Bras to buy and sell!'

My audience of bored-looking, middle-aged men took no notice. I felt that, to them, I probably looked less like an earnest commodity trader and more like a raving lunatic with an odd interest in brassieres.

A herd of black-clad widows scurried past as I barked my wares, then one turned around to peruse my pile of second-hand bras. They all came back to have a look.

'How much is this bra?' one asked me.

I told her the price.

Shocked, she said, 'Would you buy mine for that price?'

'Yes,' I responded.

She started to remove her outer jacket, then her inner garment. I eyed her in alarm; she would surely stop soon? A few seconds later, however, the bra was expertly whipped off and deposited into my sweating hand.

'Gracias,' I stuttered, embarrassed, fumbling for some coins from my pouch.

Luckily, not everyone was as brave as she. Those less audacious went home and brought back several boxes of bras. I couldn't buy them all, so I had to pick and choose. I knew I would not be able to sell them in Rabat if they were soiled, no matter what their quality.

After a full day of busy trading, the town lights came on, but the streets were still dim and spooky. Riffraff, looking for thrills, could emerge from any burrow. I ran, happy to hear my pockets jingling, from the street to the hotel. The lobby was quiet despite the soft piano music invading every corner. My soul drowned into the soothing sound.

Stretching and lying in bed, I scribbled a letter to Khadija in the hope she might read it in her dream or that some beautiful angel, or even a genie, would fly away with my words and deliver them in her peaceful sleep. My dreams were never sweet or smooth. Brawling in the street and being kidnapped or imprisoned were the recurring themes. In the daylight, in a street, café, bar, anywhere with a crowd, I tried to anticipate the faces of those with whom I might fight. I rehearsed how to duck a bullet, a broken glass bottle or a knife threat. Awake or asleep, my world was a dangerous one.

That night, for the first time, I dreamed I was flying over my enemies and dodging a bullet. I slept on my left side and awakened on the same side. Energy, I felt full of it. Hungry, I was starving. Not depressed, but frustrated.

Pattering down the stairs in the morning, I found the hotel as quiet as a cathedral, if only it had a soul. The reception was unmanned, and the lobby reeked of beer.

When I stepped out into the street, I came upon two young girls, one standing right beside the hotel door and the other leaning against the wall. They looked alike, same height and olive skin, both wearing jeans and leather jackets. They smiled at me, enticingly, but I looked away. *Professionals,* I thought cynically to myself. *Married at sunset and divorced at dawn, a short contract.*

Descending the cobbled street, I headed to the asphalt avenue to look for a bakery, but none were open. I recalled a waiter's joke: *Spanish eat late, love chickpeas and hate morning.*

Meandering, I found myself in the plaza. Here one could buy anything: bread, sausages, meat or even animal bowels. I sat in a coffee bar and pretended to smoke a cigarette to hide my provincial background. Watching the sea, I wished my energy were like the waves: never tiring. The easterly wind was sharp, fresh and reviving.

Nervous, early traders flocked in and crowded the café. Eavesdropping, I heard some people mapping their day; I saw others knotting a contract. It was a dynamic place. The talks were tough, rough, meaningful and menacing.

'Fuck off!' was never used, but 'I will cut out his tongue! He told a lie!', 'I will pull out his bowels! He took my trade!', 'I will chew off his testicles! He went to my girl!' were the words of traders.

I sipped my coffee and went back to the hotel. Reaching the entrance door, I was surprised to find the two girls still standing there. I noticed the lobby was eerily deserted, while sneaking a glance at the girls. As I passed, a whispering voice seeped into my ears.

'Boy! Can you help?'

Hesitating, I turned around and stepped out.

'Where can I get a taxi?' one of the girls asked.

'Not here. The taxi station is by the sea, a distance away,' I answered. Hearing me, the other girl broke into tears. Her companion yanked out a handkerchief and passed it to her with a tight hug.

The hug and tears puzzled me. People in this region kissed, but didn't hug. 'I can carry your case to the taxi station,' I said.

'We're boarding the ship at eleven this morning,' one of them said.

Carrying the heavy suitcase, I twisted my shoulder, but I buried my pain and saved my pride. Trailing behind them, I kept watching and wondering who they were, what they did, and where they were heading.

Reaching the plaza, I asked, 'Would you like to have a coffee?'

'Yes,' answered one of them, surprisingly.

We squeezed into a coffee bar with a vast terrace overlooking the sea. We huddled around a small table.

'We are sisters,' began Layla, who looked younger, reflective, and extremely nervous, constantly glancing sideways.

'Though this café is packed with men, it's safe,' I told her, trying to reduce her uncontrolled anxiety.

'We're not afraid of men,' said Sanaa, her sister, boldly.

'Most of these men are traders,' I told them, trying to deepen the conversation. 'They are not philanderers. They come to buy and sell, are multimillionaires, and support the entire region.'

'Illegal, though,' said Sanaa.

'Illegal? Who cares?' said Layla.

Her question and the sound of her soft-tongued voice rang a bell: Khadija. As Layla spoke, a picture began to hatch in my head. *Do I know this girl?* Beautiful hair, thick and golden, lush brows, dark brown eyes, a long face, thin, smooth cheeks, white, even teeth and a possessive smile. While she talked, I could only listen and watch. A collection of broken profiles edited itself in my mind—Soad's fiancée?

'A girl looking like you has just jilted her husband-to-be,' I said.

'Her name?' Sanaa butted in.

'Layla,' I said, remembering all Soad's photos and him cuddling the pictures.

Layla blushed and rushed to the bathroom.

'What do you do?' Sanaa asked me.

'Practically, I'm a trader. Officially, a student.'

'Strange,' she said.

'I have to finance my studies. Though I have a baccalaureate and have been unconditionally offered a place to do medicine in Belgium, I am penniless.'

Listening sympathetically, Sanaa said nothing. Silence. A gaze. Coming back, Layla broke the malaise.

'Do you know Mr Amakran?' she asked.

'Both he and his son. I was Soad's best man a few days ago.'

'I am Layla,' she said impulsively. 'With no regret, I jilted him. I'm boarding the ship in a few moments.'

She stood up and grabbed her bag angrily. Sanaa pulled her down into the chair and put an arm around her.

'What do you do?' I asked Sanaa, dispelling the storm.

'I'm a tango dancer,' she said. 'Soon I will have my own school.'

'Where?'

'In Buenos Aires, where I live.'

Feeling calmer, reassured by the love and tenderness of her sister, Layla said, 'I didn't want to get married, but my mother told me, "Spread your legs as wide as you can, close your eyes, and all will be okay." I decided it wouldn't.'

The waiter, a tall man in a white blazer, dark trousers and shoes, handed me the bill and stood waiting, dwarfing the table and us. I offered to pay the bill, but Sanaa refused.

On the way to the port along the promenade, I asked Layla, 'Are you going to Buenos Aires, too?'

'Yes,' she said.

'To do what?' I asked.

'Learn piano, express the confused sound in my head and take up painting,' she answered.

This is certainly not the girl Mr Amakran and his son Soad were expecting. How can things go that wrong and for everyone? I wondered.

As we reached the port, we found a swarm of people swathed in different clothes – reflecting different traditions, tribes and families – speaking different dialects: Tarifit, Arabic, Moroccan Darija and Spanish. Some were whispering, some were shouting and some were anxiously listening. Others were besieging the ship. We ploughed through the crowd and reached the entry to the ship. It was both magnificent and humbling, the goddess of hope. We stopped at the gangplank and gazed at each other. The two girls gave me a warm, tight hug and boarded the ship, vanishing into the crowd. I went back, weaving through the streets to the hotel. *What would Mr Amakran do or think if he knew?* I could only guess.

As the afternoon began, the street swelled with men, women and traders. As a tradition, some came out to watch and others to do rudimentary business. Some were selling eggs, and others, items of third- and fourth-hand. I saw a man shouting to sell rusty hinges.

It was a lucky trading day. I bought hundreds of knickers, some better than others, thanks to prostitutes, who were choosy and had good taste.

Budgeting ahead with my mind full of knicker sales, I thought I had enough to live on for three or four months at the university, but what after?

4

Back at home, the air was fresh, clean and cold that early dawn, mid-September, 1965. Nearly ready to go to the university, with very little money but with many bras, I went to say goodbye to Uncle Mimoun.

Unexpectedly, he asked me to accompany him to a *zawiya* for a spiritual retreat. At first, I refused, but because of what he meant to me, I reluctantly acquiesced.

'Which *zawiya*?' I asked with goosebumps. I had heard of many and hated them all. I knew Uncle Mimoun suffered from an excess dose of religiosity. After all, telling me music emanated from the throat of Satan, he had once destroyed my flute.

* * *

WHEN THE TIME CAME TO go, Mimount baked two loaves of bread, mainly barley, and boiled a few eggs. We left the house, the tribe, the family and walked two hours to catch the coach to the *zawiya*. I hated the path, the dust, the hill and the earth scratched with rivulets bearing witness to the force of torrential rain that had hit after a drought. Finally, we boarded the coach. From Zaio, we moved east toward the Algerian border, through Sabra. Several hours in a dilapidated coach made me feel sick and purposeless.

Each time I peered through the window, I saw only dust wafting through the air, a few huts dotted here and there. I tried to converse with Uncle Mimoun, but he was stone-faced.

'How long are we going to stay?' I asked. 'Not too long?' I added, hoping to defrost him. It was five in the afternoon when we were finally dropped in the desolate wilderness. The sun was down and the clouds were hovering over us.

'This is our path,' said Uncle Mimoun.

Yours, not mine, I told myself.

It was narrow, dusty and full of sharp little stones. Slowly, we climbed toward the *ʒawiya*. One hour and a half on our feet took the better of me, and there was no conversation to sweeten the journey. He probably felt I was unhappy, but then I thought he was stupid.

From far away, I spied the *ʒawiya*. Its silhouette with many mosaic additions loomed large on the darkened horizon. There were a few trees on one side.

'There it is!' I said to Uncle Mimoun. He raised his head, checked and smiled. When we arrived, we passed through a small door, and there were no trumpets or drums. The building was square, composed of about twenty-five rooms. A big cemented reservoir four metres long and five metres deep occupied the centre of the courtyard. Gullies were leading into the reservoir from all sides, and a lattice top with a hole in the middle allowed the residents to drop their buckets into the water and tug them back up. It was so quiet that the silence hit me like a smack. I looked in every direction to make meaning of where Uncle Mimoun and I had landed. I felt lost in space, time and purpose.

Exploring. Rooms with very tiny doors stood facing each other; the largest room with a full window was the residence of the holy man, or *the monster*, I thought. Whirling left and right, I saw all doors were closed. Hearing me speaking to Uncle Mimoun in the middle of the courtyard, some disciples emerged, two or three from each room. To them, we were alien. We were encircled, but not 'booed'. The look of them was threatening, and they were of all different ages, but had no women among them. Some were grim, some passively resigned. Two old men were particularly noisy and crude.

'You are here to learn what neither school nor the world have taught you,' one of them told me.

Another said, 'You won't learn anything new, but you might dispossess what the world has put into you. You can become clean and light. You might even fly like a golden eagle in the air.'

'I am just here to accompany my uncle,' I told him.

'Just, just,' he murmured.

Looking unhappy, he scurried to his room. I felt a physical urge to leave, then I cooled down, for I would have to cross several mountains and ravines in the darkness of night, and who might I meet? The monsters outside might be worse than the ones inside the walls.

Gazing at the moon, we sat on the steps in the courtyard and waited for the master, the sheik. Thick clouds veiled the moon, and the darkness tightened its grip on us. I couldn't see Uncle Mimoun, yet I felt and heard his breathing. A dim candlelight peeked out of the cracks in the doors.

In the darkness and cold, we heard a rippling, nervous thumping on a small, narrow side door beside the holy man's chamber. The thumping was to announce his arrival. On hearing it, the disciples jumped up on their toes and rushed to receive the sheik. Uncle Mimoun and I joined them. Silently, we all lined up and bowed. The master uttered no words, nodded and stepped in. I was the youngest among the disciples. He saw me and gave me a long look. He was a big man, as tall as heaven, his head covered with a thick, pink ribbon, the tail hanging over one ear. He was not wearing the *jellabah* I expected, but a garment with two wings like an eagle. A long, peppered beard covered both narrow cheeks, his chin and the front of his neck.

He was ushered to his room by Mr Slaiman, the oldest, most senior disciple, who opened the door for his master, handed him the key and bowed out. The other disciples scurried back to their huts, but our fate was still undecided, where we would sleep or what we would do.

Squatting in the courtyard, I hissed to Uncle Mimoun, 'Isn't this a madhouse?'

With his full strength, he punched me on the mouth and chipped one of my front teeth. I lost my temper, jumped up and instinctively lifted my fist to strike back. He quickly grabbed my legs and kissed my shoes. I felt blood pouring down my lips, but I couldn't hit Uncle Mimoun.

At that moment, carrying a lantern, the sheik emerged from his room and came to us. Uncle Mimoun stood up and bowed.

'I want to be your disciple, ordained and guided. In your light and path, I might reach the highest of all heights, fill the invisible, travel beyond the sun and moon and give my soul a place in heaven,' he said.

'Repent, repent,' said the holy man as he took off his own outer garment and threw it over Uncle Mimoun's head.

Walking in the beam glowing from his lantern, the holy man stepped into a large, impressive room. He lit several candles, sat down facing Mecca and mouthed a lengthy meditation prayer. Neither Uncle Mimoun nor I could guess when it would end, but it was tediously long.

The meditation over, the holy man picked up a hammer and repeatedly beat a metal plaque on the double French doors. Disciples from everywhere barged out of their huts and into the hall, with Uncle Mimoun and me behind. We sat cross-legged in an arch, facing the holy man who was seated on a sheepskin. There was no movement, no talking, no whispering. It was all complete silence. It felt like an addition to an already-frightening pitch-darkness covering the building.

I couldn't take my eyes off the holy man. *What is he going to do or tell us?* I wondered. Slowly, he stood up, gracefully shook his shoulders, ruffled his clothes and murmured.

I couldn't hear a word. A *cold-blooded man,* I thought. *No smile or obvious joy.* His eyes were hooked on the floor. Then he raised his voice and shouted, '*Hia Allah!*'

We all stood like a choir and repeated after him. He moved closer to us and threw his open palms up in the air. His eyes closed, his face was upturned toward the sky, but hindered by the ceiling.

'*Hia Allah! Hia Allah!*' he shouted.

One very old man could not stand. If anyone were

cursed, it should be either him or me – he was too old, I too young.

Elevated and excited to ecstasy, the disciples all stood there, palms in the air, imitating the master. When I hoped it was over, a dwarf slipped in through the back door, sat down facing us and began drumming. He injected energy and life. I was not expecting a dwarf to be that powerful and imposing. His drumming got louder and louder, faster and faster.

I wondered if such a small man could find a wife and what his children would look like. As his beating went out of control, the men repeated '*Hia Allah*!' and began to collapse, one after the other. They all ended panting on the floor, their mouths full of God's praise. The holy man was sitting cross-legged, controlled, meditating. Glancing around, I couldn't see who was alive or dead.

I deeply regretted coming here with Uncle Mimoun.

The cult ceremony ended well past midnight. Quickly, the holy man slithered away. The disciples, as if back from a spiritual hangover, awakened in the cold. My toes tingled from the cold, and my stomach rumbled. It seemed some disciples had come here to cry, some to lament and others to hurt themselves. Out of the spiritual chaos, I still didn't know where Uncle Mimoun and I would sleep.

Uncle Mimoun should have stayed home and enjoyed his wives, Mimount and Mariam. He could even sleep between them, both beautiful, though one is short and the other tall. He would manage.

Out of the blue, Kishuir, the dwarf in charge of accommodation came and told me, 'You will share a room with Sghir.'

'What about Uncle Mimoun?' I asked.

'He will share the room with me,' Kishuir replied.

Like a man pulling a camel in the desert, Kishuir tugged at Uncle Mimoun, six feet tall and Kishuir well below his knees.

In the pitch-darkness of night, I lost contact with them. In complete solitude, I didn't know what to do. Then, Kishuir came back and took me to a very small room with a low ceiling and low, narrow door. Gently and kindly, he awakened a middle-aged, bearded man.

'We have a visitor, and you have company,' Kishuir told him.

'How long have you been here?' I asked him.

'Days don't count for me. They are numbered only in heaven,' he answered.

'Where is your home?' I asked.

'I am at home,' he replied.

Is he sarcastic or philosophical? I wondered.

Like a bug in a rug, he bundled himself in a blanket, blew out the candle and told me, 'Goodnight.'

In the dark, I groped my way to the opposite corner and bundled myself in a ripped, smelly blanket. I was not suspicious or wary of him. He was not like the currency traders I had left behind.

As dawn peeked under the door, I noticed the man had two big green stones at his side. He awakened, threw his arms in the air, rolled up his blanket and sat cross-legged against the wall. He yanked a hidden pair of pliers from under his pillow and began pinching his arms, thighs and calves. Scars, bruises and infected spots dotted his skin. From time to time, he yelped. My presence didn't seem to bother him.

With the pliers in his hand, he paused, looked happy and said, 'I hope I didn't disturb you. I am a Sufi. Life means suffering, and suffering means life.' He got up and left the room.

Isn't this just a few steps away from committing suicide? While milling around outside the building, I came upon Uncle Mimoun.

'Did you have a good night?' I asked him.

'I did,' he answered.

We headed to Mr Kishuir's room and found him outside struggling to burn a few sticks to boil a kettle. He fed us with tea and a slice of bread.

'I am going to go into the repenting room for a few days,' said Uncle Mimoun.

'What is that?' I asked.

'It's an experience, an osmose between God and man. It's personal, individual and mysterious. No one can communicate or talk about it, and no one except the one experiencing it can understand it. It's above and beyond words,' explained Mr Kishuir.

I found the idea fascinating. Frightening, somehow. Some people came here to free their souls, either from wrongdoing or guilty feelings. Others, to unknot their psychological scleroses, but many came to embark on a Sufi life, flesh denial. A few, like Uncle Mimoun, came for the osmose experience.

Mr Kishuir and I accompanied Uncle Mimoun to the osmose room. It was a dungeon-like pit behind the building. The pit was open to the sky, but with a straw carpet on the top to repel the wind and rain. The entrance was like a trench secured by a solid door and an iron crossbar. It could only be opened from inside. With horror, I saw Uncle Mimoun disappear into the osmose room and the door shut behind him. Whoever was there was allowed to talk to himself, to cry, to shout as loudly as he wished. Later that afternoon, I heard Uncle Mimoun roaring like a lion, using the gift of the tongue, crying as though he were lashed, shouting, roaring with anger and reciting hymns in a harmonious state of mind.

I couldn't leave Uncle Mimoun, but neither could I stay. After two days, I amassed my strength to go home to ready myself for university. Making my escape at twilight, I walked on the right side of the ravine where there were no houses around, only hills. I heard an old man screaming. Frightened, I stopped. Then, I heard two voices and the lash of a whip. With each lash, the scream got louder.

This is an epic crime, I thought to myself.

I heard the man crying, 'My Lord! My Lord!'

'Here is your lord!' shouted the man as he hit again.

I left the path and climbed to the top of the hill. When I reached a small bush, I lit fire to it. The bush created an enormous bonfire, which I hoped would mark my presence and stop the crime.

I spent the rest of the night on the hill until dawn. Terrified, hungry and cold, I hurried home. On my way, I stopped at the house of Mr Ishan, the government informer. To avoid his dog, I shouted from the opposite hill. His daughter Rkia came out and ushered me into their guest room.

Mr Ishan didn't like nonsense and was a ruthless man. It was the first time I had been in his house. His guest room was very big and had two doors, one open to the house and the other to the outside. I found him lying against the wall, two red pillows on his lap, and a low, round table in front of him. I reported the crime to him.

He looked at me and shrugged his shoulders. *Surely, he doesn't want to hear me*, I thought.

He didn't doubt my testimony or accuse me of having a delusion. Pausing, he said, 'I am an informer. This is a petty crime. I wouldn't report that, just as I don't report domestic violence.'

5

The summer had been long, but not boring or eternal. I had traded in money, had witnessed trade in women, young and old, had seen my sister Rabbia's life shattered, and had watched Uncle Mimoun being led into a pit to rub shoulders with God. No day or night had passed without thinking of Khadija, not as an object of love, but as an angelic companion.

Rabat was my destination. What Khadija had done during the holiday, what she had decided as a career, I had no clue. Her parents hadn't enough money to send her abroad, and were not highly connected either, but still they were arrogant. They lived in Fes.

With a bag on my back, a suitcase in my hand, I arrived in Fes to spend a night and connect with Khadija. I never liked dirty hotels or whores' residences. A small hotel in the new town that I knew, along with its manageress, was my place of choice. Falling asleep wasn't my problem. All I needed was to pretend.

When I awoke in the morning, I took care of my appearance. I wore a blue shirt, newly bought in Melilla, dark, old trousers, but in very good condition, dark, laced shoes and a blue jacket I had bought and kept for a pleasant occasion. To crown my look, I almost washed my face with eau de cologne. Standing and facing a mirror, I thought, *Great!*

As I descended into the medina, I felt a change. From the present, I went back centuries in time. It wasn't a flashback, a theoretical concept, or imagination, but concrete and physical. Living in medina made one several centuries younger. One lived with the living as well as with the dead. Medina was a clock. The past was not Moroccan history; it was Moroccan life with veiled women, heavy and waddling, tiny shops, the abundance of mosques, some mischievous children in the street and hardworking artisans.

Near Khadija's house, streets were narrow and dark, like a tunnel with only a few dangling lights here and there to guide the healthy and the blind. Her home was a mid-terraced house in a narrow cul de sac. A black carved wooden door gave it a unique presence. Gung-ho, I knocked and waited. I heard voices, but no one came. I knocked again, this time with apprehension. Khadija's mother came, slowly as usual, jarred the door half-open and peered at me. *I am unwanted,* I thought.

Lips pursed, eyes flickering, she said, 'God help me!' as though I had come to seek alms.

'Is Khadija around?' I asked.

'You are not in this world,' she said. 'Khadija is a married woman. Mind your own business. Do you not have anything else to do?'

That was not what I had hoped, dreamed or expected. But having lived in Fes as a schoolboy, knowing how people traded in lies and distorted the facts, I dismissed her words.

Fired up by pride and humiliation, I went to see Rhama, a close friend of Khadija, who lived not far away. It was getting close to lunch time so she was at home, and when I knocked at the door, she was the first to it. She knew how Khadija and I had got on. She might have read something on my face or perhaps my voice betrayed me.

'Khadija is married,' she confirmed. 'She's working in the bank and married to her maternal cousin, Hamza, several years older than she, a divorcé and with two children.'

I was taken aback. Words were hard to find and the street spun. 'Would you like to come with me to see her?' I asked.

'Yes, after lunch. You won't make me miss the meal of the day,' she responded.

We met at three in the afternoon. Rhama was prompt, though I was there before her. She looked smart, beautiful, young and happy. The bank was only a stone's throw away in a terraced store-front in a very crowded area between the new town and the medina. Three employees were at the front counter behind the glass. They looked very busy, and the queue spilled into the street. A security officer was hovering by the door and sometimes in, sometimes out, policing the queue. Khadija was not at the front.

While I was wondering what was next, Rhama was whispering to the officer. 'We are here to see Khadija,' she told him.

She won his heart, and he let us into the bank manager's office. It was here where Khadija was sitting, facing her boss. The surprise was overwhelming. Khadija immediately jumped up and gave us each a hug. We exchanged more feelings than words.

She put her hands on my shoulders and asked me, 'Where have you been hiding?'

'Stuck in the north,' I answered.

'Doing what?' she asked.

'I failed to get a grant, so I've been trading, but my capital's been very thin. I've hardly made any money. . .'

Before I finished my sentence, Khadija's eyes filled with tears. I lost the power to talk. The bank manager saw the twirl of emotion and shouted to Khadija, 'I am going out and won't come back until closing time.'

All three of us sat around the table as if we were still in school, but the change was obvious. Khadija was wearing a gold belt, heavy gold bracelets, a thick ring and her face was heavily made up.

'You're not the Khadija I knew,' I said, jokingly.

'I am not the Khadija I want to be either,' she answered.

My visit did her no good; there was too much lost hope to take in.

'I'm on the bank's payroll, but don't have a job,' she said. 'I come and sit with nothing to occupy me. Not one single piece of paper on my desk. Or a pencil to scribble with. No telephone. I'm not allowed to read a book or bring a newspaper. I sit, look at the clock on the wall and count seconds and minutes. My boss isn't very busy either, but he's a real gentleman. Just like me, he gets bored. He checks his jacket pocket, opens his wallet, checks his driving licence, counts his money, makes a few phone calls, mostly to his wife.'

'Are you not bored, too, Jusef, during the long summer with nothing to do, just grilling under the sun?' asked Rhama.

'No, I do dangerous things, not to kill boredom, but to save my life and survive. I have a dream of being a doctor, learning English and being rich,' I answered.

Hearing that, Khadija collapsed over her desk, her face hidden by her hands, and sobbed. Rhama held her hand, and I put my arm around her. I didn't have the right words to say goodbye, so we just hugged. Rhama offered to stay with Khadija until her boss returned. As I left, I was convinced Khadija's chapter was closed. I was wrong.

At dawn the following day, I was on a bus heading toward Rabat. Finding accommodation would be a hill to climb. University rooms were for the privileged and the lucky. I wasn't one of them.

6

Fes and Rabat did not compare. Rabat was on the ocean; Fes was inland. The soil was different, but, more significantly, so were the people. Both harboured wealth and slums. Fes had a twisted, crafted soul. Stamped in the Middle Ages, tradition and religion were constantly on show. Fes women were pretty, but uneducated, and they could be dangerous. They swarmed like wasps and stung like scorpions. In secret collusion, Khadija had been buried under the avalanche of women's power and tradition.

Accommodation in Rabat was like catching a bird in the sky, even for the wealthy and rich. Hilton Hotel and Tour Hassan were for the super-rich, those from the Middle East and westerners. Seeking a room, I popped into every agent, but none was available.

Agdal was in the new quarter, exclusively inhabited by the French, God's chosen people. A cathedral rose in the middle to serve the faithful parishioners. Attached to the cathedral was a monastery called La Souse, a town in its own right with a huge walled garden several kilometres long and wide, and with only workers allowed inside. Attached to the monastery were eleven rooms rented to students every year, but only the lucky could get one.

Tired, I walked into La Souse. A Moroccan concierge guided me to the office of Father Giles. It was sunny, south-facing and well-furnished. The priest was in charge, but he was also the spokesman, the press officer and the decision-maker. He received me politely, but interrogated me like a criminal.

'I'm a new student and desperately looking for accommodation,' I said.

'Just one room is left, reserved for a Jewish student. I'm looking for a like mind for him. His mother is very protective. You know what's going on in the Middle East. I don't want to politicise our monastery,' he explained.

I didn't take in all that he meant. I had had zero contact with Jewish students. I wasn't living in the realm of politics, and religion was not my kingdom.

'It's good to have a Jewish student here, as all the rooms are filled with Moroccans,' he said.

It was meal time. He saw me to the door and closed his office. Saddened, I left, and I had just enough time to catch the coach to Fes.

Past midnight, I was in Fes. The city was in a coma. Only a few gangs and thieves were strolling the streets. I passed the night in the coach station, uncomfortable but safe.

Paul, a Franciscan priest, was in his garden when I rang the bell at six thirty. Opening the gate, he looked surprised and displeased.

'Le Pere Giles at La Source in Rabat is looking to find a

roommate to share accommodation with Michel, a Jewish student,' I said.

'Delicate task,' he remarked.

'I need a reference.'

'What shall I say?' he asked.

'I am not anti-Semitic,' I responded.

'It's true. You're hardworking and self-reliant,' he offered.

On the same day, before two o'clock, I was in Rabat with Pere Giles, who was reading Paul's reference, his head nodding.

They must trust each other's word, I thought. *Something rare in Morocco.* I was left alone while Pere Giles made a few phone calls next door. My suspicion was that he checked the letter was genuine, as it was typed. With a smile, he returned and handed me the key, but with many caveats. At four o'clock, I had to be in his office to meet Michel and his mother, coming from Mogador.

The accommodation was basic in itself, but for me, it was the end of a saga. My room, number eleven, was at the beginning of a narrow, tunnel-like corridor. It was dark and needed light both day and night. It had an alcove up two steps and a window at the side, facing the garden. My bed was a single, and the mattress was bumpy, old and smelly.

Before four o'clock, I had to see Frere Salvador, the accountant and financial manager, an extremely tall man who knew only business. The rent had to be paid fully and on time, my permanent nightmare.

I missed the time. I was to be in Pere Giles's office at four o'clock, but exhausted, I had fallen asleep. There was a loud rap on the door. Le Pere Giles looked unhappy. I had given the impression of being unreliable.

Michel and his mother were in the foyer waiting for me. Their car was parked in the street, but Michel's small motorised bicycle was in the garden. He looked older than me, was immaculately dressed in a brown leather jacket, navy polo neck, shiny shoes, expensive watch and several bracelets on his wrist. We could only communicate in French. Though he was born in Morocco, he spoke no Arabic or Moroccan dialect. Of course, his French was superior to mine. For him, French was his first language, but for me, the third. He used a lot of slang. Like a true Frenchman, he used his lips and shoulders to finish or to emphasise every sentence.

He wasn't tall, but rather short, with a nose that dwarfed his lips. He looked wiry, dynamic and agitated like a child. His mother was the opposite. Broad-shouldered and muscular, she looked loving and caring, full of worry about her son.

Honoured, I was asked to take them to the room. Michel, behind me, was carrying two suitcases, and his mother was carrying a box full of food: cheese, baked beans, canned meat, biscuits and many jars of coffee. Inside the room, glancing all over, she saw my suitcase open and full of bras.

Shocked and nearly stopping breathing, she glared at me. Before I could say anything, she stormed out of the room and immediately back to Le Pere Giles. Together, they climbed the stairs again and burst into the room.

'What are all those for? Do you need them?' he asked me.

'Yes, I do,' I answered.

Michel's mother gasped and glared at Le Pere Giles. I

immediately realised I was in trouble and could lose my accommodation.

'I have no grant. I am from the north and know no one in the town or in the south. I am self-funding. I trade in these to support myself,' I explained.

Le Pere Giles would have a real problem with Le Frere Salvador. He had taken me in without ensuring that I had funding. Stuck with me, Le Pere Giles took us all to his office and read aloud the reference from Pere Paul.

Calmed, but not reassured, Michel's mother looked at me with suspicion. Words of caution were given to her son. Michel wanted to face the garden and immediately occupied the window desk, putting his radio on. His mother took care of food, cleaned the sink and made his bed. Neither they nor I thought we would end the academic year still in this room.

Coming back after giving them a chance to settle, I found Michel eating his homemade sandwiches and opening a can of meat. He looked as if he were already missing his mother's care. I made tea and, offering me a sandwich, he graciously joined me.

'What are you studying?' I asked him.

'Agronomy,' he replied.

'Not medicine?'

'No, I don't like blood. I like fresh air. And you?' he asked.

'Arabic language.'

'Your desk is covered with biology, physics and statistics books,' he said.

'I can only get a grant if I do Arabic.'

'I have a grant and all my Jewish friends have got grants. My grant is a full one, but I will do only my first year. We are emigrating to Israel,' he said.

'You're having a Moroccan grant, studying on Moroccan soil to work in Israel.'

'This is politics,' he said with a smile.

It was the beginning of December, and the academic year hadn't started yet. The dean's room was like a foreign office, and the academic staff came like foreign ambassadors to be briefed and go.

As first year students, we were lost, but what was missed academically was filled politically. Socialist ideas and communist ideology were thriving. Chatting to a friend, I was told I shouldn't be in Rabat, for I had never heard of Poland and Romania, models to be emulated in his opinion.

The waste of time bothered and saddened me, for I had come to learn something – in fact, anything – but there was nothing. Completely self-funded, I had to trade. My knowledge of the town was meagre, and I had only just started trading in women's bras.

Saturday was the day of the week to trade. The market was in Bab el Had, a large, long road connecting two towns, Rabat and Sale. It also connected Fes, Meknes and Casa Blanca. Bab el Had was used heavily; the traffic was heavy and noisy. Cyclists, cars, taxis, coaches created a bottleneck, constantly jammed and polluting.

Stretching along the road stood an historic wall, divorcing the new town from the old. Coming out of the old town and getting into the new, Bab el Had was like the Suez Canal.

Women, old and young, modern and traditional, veiled and unveiled, collided there. There wasn't a much better place for me to trade and to show women what they could secretly wear to tie-up their bosoms at an affordable price.

My first day was hard. I filled a sack of bras and went to Bab el Had like a traveller. I picked a spot with heavy foot traffic and deafening noise. I spread a few dozen bras on a white sheet covering the ground. On the wall, I hung a similar amount. Taking care of size and colour, I aligned them to attract. With no one interested in pricing or buying, I sat down to read a pocket book. For an hour or so, I forgot where I was and why.

After the sun hit its zenith, people emerged from the old town just as others wandered into it. The historical town was an array of mysteries, of interest to historians, politicians and travellers. Vendors. There were many. Witches and wizards offered life change, how to find new love and get rid of decayed ones. Besides, there were some professionals, technically savvy and intellectually bright. With old typewriters, they wrote documents, letters to friends, complaints to police, court or companies.

A strolling, gazing flock of women stopped and watched me hanging bras. They nodded as they passed. Two men walking by stopped and gave me a nasty look.

'Are you allowed to trade in women's bras?' one of them asked.

'Why not?' I retorted.

'Shame! Shame upon you!' shouted the other.

They must have a pathological or perverted perception, I thought.

As more and more people descended to immerse them-selves in the bowels of the old town, the old town vomited its own. Men and women moving up and down, right and left, thronged the plaza. I didn't feel proud or ashamed, but just condemned.

A few metres away, a scribe sat on a wooden stool, an old typewriter on his table, and shouted, 'Where are you from?'

I ignored him. He had a few clients and when typewriting, he looked like a boxer. His typing sounded like a machine gun.

One tall woman, strong and rich-looking, strolling on her own, stopped, picked up and examined almost every bra on the wall and on the ground. *She has a sense of quality and detail.*

'Why are the hooks different?' she asked.

'Some come from Germany and some come from Italy,' I answered. In fact, I didn't know. I thought she was a genuine buyer, but I couldn't see her face. Just her eyes, like a snake, with a feeling of horror. Whatever price I asked, she gave me a third, a real loss for me. She haggled and tantalised me.

Listening to her, a woman passing by shouted, 'Don't let him fool you! He picked them up from the French bin!'

She made me lose a potential client. It wasn't a good day. As the sun set, the light went with it, and the bras' colours became blurry. The street was not well lit. There were just enough lamp posts to prevent collisions.

Not having sold one single bra, I wondered if I would be able to pay my way through the university. Back at the monas-tery, I found Michel and his friend Jacob, a Moroccan Jew, ready to go to the university restaurant not far away.

We all went and sat apart from the rest of the students. The Jewish students were not popular and they often stayed in a ghetto. I was mocked for sharing a room with a Jewish student, and now I was sharing a table. There was an atmosphere of anti-Semitism, but it never translated into violence.

Even with only three of us, I wasn't a part of the conversation. The topic was exclusively Israel. Michel's and Jacob's parents were on their last leg of emigration. They had sold their houses, their businesses and whatever they could. In a few months, they would be picked up via the sea by Israelis. The story seemed fictional. Curiosity and impatience got the best of me.

'Israel is not your country,' I told Michel.

Jacob jumped, kicked the floor, pounded the table and said, 'Israel is our biblical land, given to our ancestors by God.'

'But you are not in it,' I said.

'My heart is in it,' replied Jacob.

'Your ancestors have left. How can it be always yours?' I asked.

'It's a gift from God,' he said. 'It's ours. We can go and come back.'

'Arab countries have very strong armies. Joined together, they could destroy your dream.'

Michel butted in violently. 'The Israeli army is much better and much stronger than all the Arab armies put together!'

'I've never heard such things,' I said. *We've been fed by different sources,* I thought. We walked with Jacob to his room, then Michel and I returned to our own room at the monastery. The university was not in a hurry, and I was in pressing need of making some money to pay the rent to Frere Salvador and buy some food.

Day after day, week after week, month after month, the job was the same. At the foot of the mural, facing the new town, I spread a dozen bras. A similar number were hung against the wall. Though they looked like washing to be dried, they were for sale. Bras found their lovers. I sold between fifteen and twenty every afternoon.

In the midst of scribes, witches, beggars and clairvoyants, I was the most successful, to judge by the number of women crowding me to buy or simply to enjoy the bargaining. Mr Haddo, a scribe, was my neighbour. After a month of resentment and dislike, he befriended me. He came and stood beside me, either to steal my marketing skill or just watch. He often came, stood and gazed. With his typewriter, table, chair and a few stools, he had an office in the open air. He looked to be in his sixties, but he might have been younger. However, the sun, hard life and frustrations had ploughed deep furrows in his face.

'You are a typist,' I told him one day. 'You have a skill that I don't have.'

'Come and watch me,' he said.

Whenever I was free, I sat with him and watched him perform his skill. When I thought he was depressed, I brought him a mint tea. With his cigarette and his mouth almost free of teeth, his face was hardly visible when he smiled, yet he was a man of great heart.

He typed and edited curricula vitae for old and young men, some applying to the police, the army or simply the council. A middle-aged man once came and applied to be a hangman.

Mr Haddo couldn't dissuade him, so he typed and edited an application. I sometimes corrected his grammar and spelling. He could have found a job as a civil servant if it had not been for his age and his looks.

He once invited me for Friday couscous. He and his four girls lived in a hovel, hard to find and reach. His oldest, Yamina, was eleven. He never mentioned his wife nor did his daughters mention their mother.

She has either died or left, I thought. *They will be expecting a gift from me, but all I have is a sackful of bras.*

Yamina acted as a housewife, mother and sister. She looked pleasant, but weary, with burdens beyond her age. She had either learned or was told how to smile. She invited her father to sit as if he were a visitor. While we sat, she gave orders to her sisters as if they were monkeys. She brought us a big plate of couscous, but without meat.

The four girls sat with us. We all dipped from the same plate. 'Let us stop and let our father and his guest finish their meal,' Yamina ordered her sisters.

My heart melted.

'No,' I insisted. 'If you stop, we all stop.'

They looked surprised.

Mr Haddo hadn't provided a decent lodge for his girls, nor enough food, but he hadn't sold any of them or given them as maids. He went to work and came sometimes with a day's living and sometimes not. He provided a poncho of love. They weren't in the street under the rain, nor in the queue with beggars. But in Mr Haddo's love, there was a big crack: the absence of school. He blamed poverty.

'No! Poverty is an effect, not a cause,' I told him.

He grimaced.

* * *

THE FACULTY OF ARTS STARTED in mid-December, but there was no academic staff to guide it. Sporadic hours were filled with secondary teachers. Jokes and laughs filled the classes. This did not justify the hardship I'd undertaken to get there, I believed, but others found it to be a good time. The number of girls didn't match the number of boys, so the competition was fierce.

You'd had it if you lacked money and good looks. I had neither. Living in a convent in a Muslim country, sharing a room with a Jewish boy and selling bras, made me odd. Michel befriended a boy from Norway named Paul. He was tall, blond and also rich and smart. He had come to read French and Arabic, had an interest in architecture and wanted to write a book. His visits were frequent and sometimes inconvenient. When Michel was not in the room, I taught him Arabic, yet I never understood why anyone should come to an African country to learn a language with little practicality.

Paul rented a room in a big villa on a prestigious street. His landlord was a French lady, Madame Givenchy. She didn't like visitors and owned a horrible dog. She thought all Moroccans were liars, thieves, unreliable and not worthy of respect. That was why she would never rent a room to them, she had told Paul. I once dropped by to see him, and her unleashed dog behind the gate nearly grabbed me. I won over the dog and rang the bell.

Furious, Madame Givenchy came out of the house, stood behind the gate and shouted, 'Look what you have done to my dog! You rendered him mad!'

'In Morocco, a person is more important than a dog!' I retorted. For her, I was less. 'I've come to see Paul.'

'I'm not in charge of Paul's time and life,' she said.

On the same day in the evening, Paul came by to see Michel, but Michel was in Mogador. I offered Paul coffee and spent an hour talking.

Tired of my room with its two beds, he invited me to his room in the luxurious villa. On our way, he bought a bottle of red wine and a tin of sardines. His room was stunning with big windows, a sofa, armchairs and a huge bathroom. We both drank coffee, listened to classical music and read the newspapers. Paul disappeared into the bathroom. I heard water running and thought it was to clear the air. Then I realised he was taking a bath.

'Jusef! Jusef!' he called to me with a cheerful voice. Hesitating, I opened the door. He was completely naked with his bottom facing me and the bathroom full of perfume. I backed out, but he called me again.

'Would you like to have sex with me?' he asked.

Horrified, I stood as if in a trance. I stumbled backwards. He called me again.

'No! Put your clothes on and come out!' I shouted.

Gracefully, he did. We had a second coffee.

When Michel came back, Paul was a permanent visitor, but I felt constantly embarrassed. I wondered whether other people knew and if they did, what they thought.

At Christmas, we holidayed as Christians. New Year came, and we did the same. Still, the faculty wasn't sure what to teach us. To fill a gap, an Egyptian came and lectured us on the origin of man: monkeys, he concluded. After an hour of lecture, we never saw him again. He was a diplomat.

After many blank days, Professor Bradda came. The Arabic novel was the topic, but he was cynical and sarcastic. He poked fun at every religious figure, mocked every revered word and peered from behind his desk to see our reactions. It was a time of disrespect for religion and Moroccan tradition. It was also a time of ideology.

Le Pere Giles was just the opposite. He embarked on instilling social care in us and organised small talks and seminars. He invited several speakers; most of them were rich and Catholic. He invited a devout couple, and the topic was 'Love and Divorce'. While talking, the speaker, Peter, held his wife's hand. We were expecting to hear about romance in France and, in particular, Paris. It was there where lovers kissed and their social honour remained unharmed.

We were puzzled and disappointed when he turned out to be a missionary.

'No sex before marriage,' he told us. 'No divorce. If divorce is granted, neither one should remarry.'

Sex before marriage was not difficult for us to understand, but not divorce. 'Wouldn't the divorce be just as sweet as the first love?' I asked him.

'No,' he said.

'Like flowers with no scent, my sisters know a lot about sex, have never spoken of love and are not ashamed. They are like a screw in the wall. Divorce would be just like extracting a rotten tooth,' I explained.

'I am telling you what God says,' he replied.

Le Pere Giles didn't like my challenging the speaker.

'I spoke from experience, and the speaker spoke from the book,' I told him.

Zealous, Le Pere Giles tried various speakers. Mr Kat was invited as a star. He veered from the topic and went to politics.

'Socialism is what we need,' he said.

Le Pere Giles stood up and went berserk. He stopped the speaker and ended the talk. Half of the audience, though students, were informers. This night marked the end of Le Pere Giles's ambition.

7

Bras were popular with women, both old and young. But, as I ran out of them, I ran out of food. Frere Salvador might have been on a good tie with God, but not with everybody. To collect the rent, he acted like a prison officer with no mercy or charm. The rent had to be paid in full and on time. I skipped many lunches to save my pride and avoid his wrath.

I thought of travelling north to Melilla, Spain, to restock bras. The region was poor, but dynamic. Rabat was economically dead, a town of civil servants, shirts and ties. But, travelling north exacted money and time. Second-hand bras could only be bought in Melilla where Spanish women and chic prostitutes could afford new bras and disposed of the old. My market was limited, but ironically, it was only over precious fabric and style where women, rich and poor, old and young, pious and perverted, met.

Tormented, I didn't want to abandon my lectures, though mediocre, and looked for a part-time job. *I'm good at maths*, I thought. *Why not find a job in the banking sector?* Smart, with a shirt and tie, I went to the biggest bank on the main avenue.

'May I speak to the manager?' I asked a girl.

'Why?'

'I'm looking for a part-time job,' I responded.

'Ha! Ha! Ha! He's in a meeting!'

In fact, he was not there at all, I learned after fierce insistence. Other banks were no more receptive to my enquiries. Just as the street was saturated by strollers, the banks were with employees. My maths didn't serve me well.

A butcher trading in horsemeat offered me an afternoon job on Fridays so that he could go to the mosque and sleep the rest of the day. Sadly, I wasn't a good surgeon.

I awakened one morning and began to knock on every French villa in Agdal. At one big house on the corner, I smelled French coffee before ringing the bell.

The French woman confused me with her maid and shouted, 'Fatima! You are too early today. I haven't finished my coffee.'

As she opened the gate, I said, 'I'm buying old books and magazines. Do you have any?'

'People are coming here asking for clothes, not books and magazines,' she told me in an unfriendly voice.

Hearing my voice, her husband shouted from the balcony, 'Shut the gate and let him go!' She shut the door and secured the lock.

Moving to the next villa, I found it even harder. A fierce dog, detecting my presence, barked and tried to jump the wall. I dared not reach the gate, let alone ring the bell.

My morning was a complete failure. Frustrated, I felt like a beggar. For a week, I did nothing but think of how to get out of the rut and not have to abort my academic year.

One morning, on my way to the faculty, I met a student friend picketing. He tried to hand me a bunch of leaflets, but I refused.

He saw the problem in politics, but I saw it in society, mentality, family.

'If you give one billion to each man and woman today, tomorrow you will see them the same,' I told him.

He didn't like what I said, nor did I like what he did.

Having no choice, I resumed knocking on every French villa. I changed the time and tactic, however. I avoided the morning, as I couldn't deal with the French wrath and insults.

I began knocking in the afternoon, after lunch. For whatever reason, wine, food, tiredness, many women were civil. I knocked on a villa in Les Oranges. A woman called me from behind the gate. She was short and plump, with beautiful silver hair. She sounded lonely and happy to chat.

'Books and magazines to sell?' I asked her.

She invited me into her front garden. As I stood facing her, she leaned against the wall. 'What type of books?' she asked.

'Any.'

'Magazines?' she asked.

'*Paris Match*.'

She asked me into her library. *She must have been a teacher*, I thought, *or an academic*. Piles of books were scattered all over the floor. Sacks of magazines and newspapers filled every corner. Some looked new, others, dusty and cobweb-laden. She only wanted to get rid of certain books, a mishmash of titles. Bargaining was difficult. She wanted full price for every book. I tried to charm her, but failed to win.

'What do you want those books for?' she asked.

'To resell them,' I said. That hardened the bargaining and her heart.

'Every book has a soul,' she said.

I knew that couldn't be true. Cafes and restaurants ripped books apart and used them in the toilets in the absence of water. I bought thirty books and picked the smallest in size. Her piles of magazines were as high as a ladder, and she wanted to get rid of them.

'I buy only *Paris Match*,' I told her.

'*Paris Match* isn't for the brainy,' she said.

'You bought it.'

She paused. 'I like to browse. I like to gaze at a handsome, beautiful man, smart and rich. There aren't many in this land.'

What about me? I thought to myself. *I'm not well-dressed, but pretty okay.* I trudged back with a heavy load of *Paris Matches* and felt like a donkey. I carried books and magazines, but had no idea what was inside. I came upon Le Pere Giles at the monastery gate.

Looking at me, he said, 'Are you going to read all those magazines?'

'No, they are for sale,' I answered.

'Who would buy them?' he asked.

'Moroccans,' I said.

'Those are luxury magazines, not educational.'

'Pleasure and education don't go hand in hand,' I responded.

Knocking on doors to buy second-hand books and magazines almost became my main job and means of survival.

The spot where I had sat and spread bras near Mr Haddo was still unoccupied. He was pleased to see me back.

I spread *Paris Match* and different books on the ground at Bab el Had (Sunday Gate), but never the Bible, the Holy Koran or any theological, religious or political book. *Paris Match* was full of beautiful romantic pictures: men and women smiling, meeting, wealthy and happy. I opened several pages so everyone could stop and look.

With bras, I had attracted only women, but now both men and women were interested, and of all ages. They came to browse, picking up and flicking through the pages. Some bought one and some bought more. I noticed, however, the absence of the older women. Books, despite the variety and the price, didn't attract them.

'Reading is a hard job,' a young man told me.

'French isn't my mother tongue,' another told me.

By this time, I had a trusting relationship with Mr Haddo. I liked watching him type and he liked to browse through my magazines for free. Through him, I met an old teacher who owned his own house but took lodgers.

For a fraction of what I had paid to Le Pere Giles, I joined three other students. Also, by this time, the relationship between Paul and Michel had been getting closer and closer.

In sadness, I told Frere Salvador, 'I am not able to meet the rent.' I handed him the key, and there were no words from either of us.

In my new home, which dated from the Middle Ages, five of us shared one bathroom. Two were in each room, and the landlord occupied the lounge for himself alone. The bathroom was often blocked and backed up. The landlord was amiable, but lazy, and the house was crumbling, doors and walls giving up their form.

Whenever I was in business, Mr Haddo called me to correct his Arabic. He called me once and gave me the impression he was in distress. I found a woman sitting beside him. I noticed there wasn't much conversation between them. She looked to be in her late thirties, beefy and strong, with no head scarf or veil, and had asked him to write a divorce document on behalf of her daughter, married to a policeman.

'I want him to divorce my daughter,' she kept repeating. 'I want to disgrace him at home, among his friends and in the court.'

'What is the basis of this divorce?' Mr Haddo asked.

'He broke the marriage convention. He committed adultery. He . . . only has anal sex with my daughter.'

We were both numbed. Mr Haddo couldn't find the right words to write. He struggled.

'Just write what she said,' I told him.

* * *

THERE WERE TOO MANY STRIKES to count them all, but the spring one was dangerous, close to exam time. There was a risk that the entire year could be dismissed. For those on grants, it meant a double calamity: the loss of the academic year and the grant. Along with many, I opposed the strike, and we went back to the lecture theatre. We were caught between the Islamists and the ultra-bolshevists.

Before the exams, the weather changed; the air was warm

and the days were hot and agreeable. Any ground unspoiled by litter or buildings was green and peppered with white, pink and red flowers. All that was not of much help. A wave of anxiety washed over my heart and mind. I might or I might not pass my exams. The Arabic language, beautiful as it was, was not my choice, but I didn't want my lack of choice to be my reason for failure. I slept so little, obsessed with catching everything I might have missed.

With all the fever of exams, the Jewish students organised a night of dancing, and Michel invited me. The dance was in Agdal, and I lived in the bowels of the town. Only loonies could cross from the old to the new town at night. As I was always attracted by beautiful girls, it was a unique chance to talk and dance with some charming Jewish girls, most of them studying exclusively medicine or economics.

The house was big and packed with boys and girls. Night came and the confusion started. The music was not Moroccan. It was jazzy, Chicago inspired. Everybody was polite, but the crowd was cliquey. After a short conversation, everyone politely got rid of me. Maybe I wasn't a marriage candidate.

A girl, not keen to dance, kept talking to me, and I kept going back to her. Paul joined us. With him, the conversation changed. Clare, doing medicine, was truly a Jewish girl. She spoke about medicine and Israel. I was neither informed nor interested. She mapped her future in the Middle East; Paul was a dedicated artist. Both of them glorified their historicity.

I had my own, but it was negative: no school and no food. It wasn't the Spanish's fault, French's fault, Japanese's fault. It was my parents', grandparents' and great-grandparents'. The chain was long. The solution for me was not to doubt everything, as Descartes had, but instead to reject everything: no past and no present, just the future. It was there where I wanted to be, not where my parents had been nor where I was now.

On the eve of the exams, I was possessed by an insomnia that I had never experienced before. Having five people in a squashed house didn't help. Doors slammed, some boys whistled and others yelled. There were no rules or order. The night didn't mean rest or silence, just a change of light. The landlord had a television and radio and was constantly browsing for news; late stations were the worst. To escape the misery of my first exam night, I spent the rest of them with a friend supported by seven brothers.

Not knowing what to expect, I passed my exams, but Michel failed. Hearing the news, I went to see him. I found him calm and reflective.

'I am anxious,' he told me. 'I have to resit my exams and prepare myself for a new life in Israel. I have to learn Hebrew and find my way.'

'You have failed your exams and know what to do. I passed mine, but I don't know how to do what I want to do: medicine,' I said.

'You love biology,' he said. 'Push.'

'You need a free space to push into and a stick to push with. I have no money,' I told him.

Paul arrived and we all went to a café in Agdal. 'The dancing night was great, wasn't it?' Paul asked me. 'Have you fallen in love with anyone?'

'No,' I said. 'And you?'

'I have fallen in love with all of them.'

'Wow!'

As he was so attentive, I told him, 'I had a sweetheart, Khadija, in Fes. She and I were so close, and we were supposed to be in the same university, somewhere. When I went home during the holiday, I worked as a currency trader. It was a very tough job, among dangerous gangs. Going back, I found Khadija married to her cousin. I was faithful and she wasn't.'

Suddenly, Paul burst into tears. I kept silent and, in a trance, kept watching him. He wiped his tears, cleared his nose and said, 'I am an artist. Morocco has given me a lot to write about and paint. I am going to be very, very busy.'

'There aren't many people who are artists like you,' I told him.

'Wrong. Moroccans are natural artists and intelligent, too. I am a member of a men's club. We meet each week. We listen to music through the night, we throw our clothes off and discover each other as well as discover who we are,' he told me.

'Isn't that a sin?' I asked him.

'No, it's art.'

'Paul, be what you are and let me stay where I am,' I told him.

8

After a summer trading chickens and eggs at home in Kebdana, I went back to Rabat, where I knocked, searched and looked everywhere for a grant. Michel was already back from Mogador to resit his exams, and I met him afterwards. Most of his relatives had already emigrated to Israel. Left alone, he was waiting to gain some qualification before joining his family.

When he passed his exams, we celebrated in a café. He was in no real hurry to go, and when the moment came to leave, he began to cry.

'Why?' I asked him. 'You are going to a much better place, the land of Abraham, Jacob, David.'

He paused, breathing heavily, and said, 'I love Morocco.'

'So do I,' I told him.

'I will spend a few months in a kibbutz,' he said.

The name didn't mean anything to me. Leaving him at the coach station, I went to the German embassy. I had heard and read that country was rich, offered grants, and its educational system offered the opportunity for a part-time job.

The cultural attaché offered no help.

'Though plenty of jobs are available in school, there is no

contract between Morocco and Germany. Just between France and Germany. You are excluded anyway,' he said. 'Whenever we offer a grant, we offer it to the Moroccan authorities. They decide who gets it.'

Having explored every avenue and failed at each step, I decided to carry my fate on my own shoulders. I wrote a letter to Mr Ali, working and residing in Germany. 'May I stay with you a few days?'

Mr Ali's wife and children lived in Morocco, in Zaio. It happened once that one of his sons had been critically ill. The boy's mother, uneducated, never allowed outside the house, had watched her son, like a candle, being extinguished before her eyes. When I saw the boy, just a toddler, I had offered to take him to the doctor. He was diagnosed with pneumonia, and the antibiotics worked their miracle. Mr Ali and his wife never forgot that I had saved their son.

After I bought the train ticket to travel from Rabat to Frankfurt, I was left with only three hundred dirhams. In Melilla, I knew my way – streets, hotels, who to trust and how to be suspicious – but not on a ship. Packed, the ship gave the impression of losing its balance from the start. Floors and seats were full; there was nowhere to sit. I kept wandering. Spanish people were loud and cheery; the rest, mostly Africans, looked depressed. I wondered if they knew where they were going. I filled my mind with some creative imaginings: some travellers were emigrants, job-hunters, some were criminals, escaping prison and justice. It was unlikely there were any lovers.

The ship lilted with the wind and waves, and many started to throw up. A smell of cheese and beer came out, and so did the couscous. I took refuge in a small corner and hunkered down on the floor to avoid human contact and smells, but I felt very cold, freezing. I woke up to the sound of the ship's horn.

Anchored at the port, the ship needed permission to unload. The waiting time was nerve-wracking. Excited Spaniards began shouting and, sometimes, singing. The mood vacillated just like the waves under the ship.

When the door opened, the gangplank was connected to the dock. We were all swept out; my first steps on European soil were into the clutches of the border police. As they strained us, the queue stretched and overflowed the building. A policewoman picked me out, searched my suitcase and found nothing. She waved me on.

I boarded the train and sat down, but it didn't want to move. Travellers, mainly Spaniards, filled the train and brought their food: bread, sausages and wine. No one seemed to be in a hurry, anxious or bored. They just sat cheerfully, drank and talked. The train seemed to be a meeting place rather than a moving vehicle. I knew it would take twenty-four hours to reach Madrid. As a novice traveller, I was unprepared. When the train moved, an undercover policeman stood up and checked our IDs. Satisfied, he left.

The train was slow, and, looking right or left, the beauty of the land could only be described as 'Andalucía'. It was a hub of ancient civilisations and culture, where Muslims had once come and prospered but been swept away and wiped out. The rolling hills, covered with olive trees, were mind-capturing. The slowness of the train was almost desirable, planned to let the curious eyes be captured by this brown land, reflecting what the sun had to offer. This was winter. I wondered what the spring would be like? *If I were a painter or poet, I would reside here.*

The train was not only slow. It stopped where one wouldn't expect or want. It stopped in every little village, each one showing a different colour of Spain; no two were ever the same. Madrid seemed to move farther away, never nearer. Relaxed, passengers left the train and came back with either food or drink.

In the middle of the journey, a woman joined our compartment. She was broadly built and had two children on each side. One was wearing old, broken and shabby shoes. *Franco, along with Hitler, has robbed this beautiful family of their freedom and dignity,* I thought. My shoes were not much better, but that was not what I had been expecting. When it came time to feed her children, she included me. She handed me a roll of white bread and a dried sausage, a food that, as a Muslim, I could not enjoy without regret. I kept the bread and handed the sausage back to her. She understood. Then, she passed me a piece of cheese.

Malaga and Madrid were not identical twins or even biological ones. They were just different. I didn't have a chance or the guts to go far into Madrid, but I left the station and peeked out. Being far from the sea and not industrialised made the capital white, as white as snow.

On the train, I found myself with a group of young Spanish lads acting up. They had started drinking at dawn and looked shabby and unkempt. Each one was hugging a big bottle of wine. I would have preferred to be in a different compartment. They talked, laughed and paused. Then, the ringleader began to revive his comrades. Talking, laughing, he lost his mind. He faced his friends and began masturbating.

It was a great relief to reach Hendaye, a small town on the French border. The contrast between Spain and France was stark. There was a difference in prosperity and wealth. Houses were bigger and detached. The gardens and the red roofs added colour.

French soil was not open to all, and the border was like a piece of iron. The North Africans were scanned like plague. Five Moroccans who had been refused entry sat huddled together licking their fate with no straw to grab. My luck wasn't happier. The officer browsed over my passport and checked my ticket. Puzzled, he called his senior, a middle-aged man.

'Where are you going?' he asked me.

'Germany, sir.'

'To do what?'

'Work and study.'

'Do you have a grant?' he asked.

'No.'

'Do you have a visa?'

'No.'

'Do you have any contract?'

'No.'

'Do you have any college acceptance? Do you have money to live on?'

'Three hundred dirhams.'

'Do you have any address where you're going?'

'I have some friends.'

'Do you know their address?'

'No. I will look for them.'

'I regret I will not let you in. Do not stamp his passport,' he told his junior. I stepped back, then went back to him as he was still standing there. I showed him my ticket.

'I am not intending to stay in France,' I told him.

He browsed the ticket again, nodded his head and said with a fake smile, 'I've seen similar to this. Paris is already full. I can only let you go if you have a return ticket, which you don't have.'

I stepped back again.

The border between France and Spain was not an iron curtain. A trafficker was already waiting to take unsuccessful people like me from the border to drop them somewhere on French soil, far away from the border. Three of us jumped into his hired taxi, were driven and dropped in the countryside. From nowhere, I began hitchhiking. There were very few cars and for hours, no one stopped. Most cars were Deux Chevaux, Citroen.

A couple passed me and later came back to give me a lift to the station. Without a stamped passport, I boarded a train.

I arrived at Frankfurt Allgemeine train station at four in the afternoon, late December. No one was expecting me, and I expected no one to meet me. The station was big, and so were the men and women milling in and out. It was noisy and busy. When I sat to have a coffee, I was ignored, and the ground shook under my feet like an earthquake. It was bright inside, but pitch-dark outside.

I ventured out to discover where I had landed. The bright sun and the fresh air were far behind in Morocco. The sky was misty and dripping, and the air heavy and filthy. My lungs tightened and my nose began to drip.

I left the station with no route in mind, but directed myself toward the centre of town. The street was large, but not special. Everybody wore a coat, some carried umbrellas, but I had only a light summer jacket made in Morocco. Heading deeper, coming closer into the city centre, I came upon small road-works. Some workers were mixing the cement and some were hammering to patch the potholes in the street.

Horror! I spied a young man from my tribe converted into a donkey. A thick, long stick ran behind his neck, and two steel buckets hung like saddlebags from the ends. Filled with steaming, nearly burning, cement, the buckets were carried from here to there. Mesmerised, I stood watching him. I thought this was a land of technology. Could they not use a wheelbarrow instead of humanity? Was it worth smashing a man's neck to smooth the street?

Back at the train station and wondering if I should head to Paris, I noticed a small flock of men around a table. They looked happy, close-knit and whispering. I was delighted to see some brown skin and dark-haired men speaking in a language I understood. With no invitation, I joined them. Soon, they realised I was a traveller.

'Are you meeting someone here?' one asked me.

'No. Do you know Mr Ali from Zaio, Beni Sa Tout tribe?'

'Of course!' shouted one of them. 'In a minute, he will be here. We gather here, talk, exchange job information and look for family news.'

Mr Ali arrived, accompanied by his brother, Tahar. We

exchanged hugs and took a new table. A waitress, tall and broad, stood by our table to take our order.

'*Un coffee pour moi*,' I said.

Ali ordered a beer, an espresso and a glass of water. Then, from his pocket, he yanked a cigar that filled his mouth and lips. I had never seen a cigar before, nor knew what it was for. This was not the Mr Ali I knew: pious, never a cigarette in his mouth, let alone alcohol. I wondered if he still prayed or went to the mosque.

Watching me wondering, he said, 'No path of joy should ever be barred.'

'Where to stop?' I asked him, grinning.

'Your body is self-driven. It will tell you. If you don't listen, it will do it for you. Let the blood-energy move and dance with it, not against it.'

I realised that Mr Ali and I were not in the same world, though we were in the same country, town, station and around the same table. I was overloaded with recipes: no alcohol, no pork and fast, no matter how hard it might be. Some recipes were religious, some parental and others of my own making. I had come to Germany not to change my skin, religion or culture, but in the hope of financing my university studies.

Mr Ali was generous despite his brutal divorce from everything that I knew. I asked to stay with him a few days or weeks, and he agreed.

It took us about twenty minutes on the train to reach where he lived. It was not a house, bungalow, flat or tent; it was a hut with more than three bunk beds inside. However, it was warm, with electricity and water and a toilet outside. It was in a ghetto of huts. That was what the rail company provided for its workforce.

Ali, his brother, Tahar, and others were happy despite missing their families and Moroccan culture. I lived with Ali and Tahar for three weeks and slept on the floor. It was a ghetto with no osmose between the German communities and them.

Like a duck, I began to fly on my own. Ali and his friends were too close. They worked together, shopped together and went to the brothel every Friday as a group. Each one of them knew his lover, and no switching was allowed.

I went with them to a posh bar once. Several women were hovering about. Ali and his friends all ordered beer or liquor, but I asked for a coffee.

The woman danced around and said, 'Coffee! Coffee! Coffee! What a man! Only mighty and strong men come here!'

'This place,' Tahar told me, 'is to lose your brain, not to retrieve it with coffee.'

When I got to know the town and the tram, I went to the University of Frankfurt and asked to be registered on one of their special programmes to learn German. *The beginning of the beginning*, I thought.

The office was big, and a row of women were at the front desk protecting the boss behind them. He emerged from the back, looking strong but tired, and asked to see my passport. He thumbed through it and asked if I had had any education.

I showed him my baccalaureate and my first year's transcript from Rabat University. He slammed my passport on the counter and said, 'You need a police stamp.'

'Do I need a police stamp to learn German?' I asked him.

He shouted, yelled and pushed me out. 'Go back to your country! Go back!'

'Go back!' fell on my head like a pickaxe. Naively, I thought the university was full of good, polite people.

I went back to the Moroccan ghetto outside Frankfurt to talk to Tahar and Mr Ali. It was past 9 p.m. when I arrived. The ghetto was dark, ghost-like and spooky. Disappointed, I found neither Mr Ali nor Tahar in the hut.

While I was waiting, a big man emerged from a hut nearby. As he saw me, he raced at me with a kitchen knife in his hand.

I am going to be stabbed! I was afraid, but I didn't run so I wouldn't give him the impression I was a thief or an intruder.

'Hello! Hello!' I shouted at him in French. He didn't respond. I couldn't remember ever seeing a man that broad with such excessive muscles and stomach.

'Mr Ali! Tahar!' I shouted, trying to sound familiar.

When he came near, he shouted in French, 'You're not allowed here!'

'I'm looking for Mr Ali and Tahar,' I responded.

'Do you know them?' he asked.

'Yes,' I answered.

'If you do, why did you come when they are not here?'

'I didn't know that,' I said.

'Why do you come at night?' he asked.

'It's now that I need them.'

'What for?'

'To borrow some money,' I responded.

Suddenly, he dropped his knife down by his side, put his other hand on my shoulder and went back to his hut. I sighed with relief as he switched on his light.

Tahar and Mr Ali both arrived late, waddling with shopping bags. Tahar was a unique soul. He didn't believe in God, but in good.

As we finished breakfast in the morning, I asked Tahar, 'Could you lend me one thousand deutschmarks?'

Though I had saved Mr Ali's son's life, I didn't dare ask him. I knew the type of heart he possessed.

But on hearing me ask Tahar, he jumped and shouted, 'You have just arrived!'

'Renting a room and being registered with the police is a prerequisite to entering the university,' I told him.

A long silence filled the room with stillness. With a fixed look and a smile, Tahar said, 'You have it. One thousand deutschmarks.'

That morning changed my night. I had been drowned in a dream of boxing with no gloves, of receiving punches, but I had been locked in the ring. The referee had seen that I was beaten but hadn't stopped the fight. I was glad that the morning erased my dream.

Tahar and I left the hut and went to the bank in the centre of Frankfurt where he handed me one thousand deutschmarks. Immediately, I began hunting for a room to rent. I visited every address that was mentioned in the local newspaper. The best of them was a narrow corridor with no light or water, but just a dim light farther down the corridor and a dirty sink with a dripping pipe. Seemingly unaware of what she was offering, the lady was arrogant.

Residual from the Second World War, I thought.

Not happy with my disgust, she said, 'Do Africans have much better?'

Frustrated, I went back to stay with Tahar and Mr Ali. Not finding a room and the borrowed money beginning to dwindle, I decided to buy a tent and live far away from the town. Neither Mr Ali nor Tahar knew my intention. Not knowing either Frankfurt or its suburbs very well, like a gypsy I took a bus to hunt for a safe and free spot to pitch my tent, which I hadn't yet bought.

I ended in a forest, not knowing whether it was south, north or east of Frankfurt, and there I found a group of five men planting trees. They had both light and heavy lorries with full equipment to dig in the forest.

'Are you looking for a job?' one of the men asked me.

'Yes.'

The man looked to be in his fifties and seemed decent and believable. He was giving orders to others, wearing a hardhat on his head and boots on his feet.

How lucky! I thought to myself. *I've found a job and place to pitch a tent.* I was assigned to dig one hundred holes, plant a tree and fill it again. It was like what the French army called a 'chore.' Yet, I liked the job. I dug and enjoyed the challenge. I planted more than all of the others put together, as they spent most of the time talking and drinking beer. They were pleased, and so was I. By the time we stopped at four thirty, my trousers were destroyed and my shoes drowned in mud.

I asked the chief, 'How will I get paid?'

'We work for the council,' he said. 'We will give you a voucher and the timetable. The council will pay you.'

Muddy, I took a bus heading to the shantytown to spend the night with Tahar and Mr Ali. I was lucky that both of them were at home, cooking Brussels sprouts and chicken. Neither Mr Ali nor Tahar liked my dirty state.

I worked four days in the forest, digging holes and planting trees. The other men did some work, but spent most of their time inside their vans, drinking, smoking and flicking through pornographic magazines.

While my body was sweating, my mind was wondering. *This is a beautiful spot for a tent.* At noon on Friday, the job seemed to be finished, and the foreman gave me a voucher to pick up my wages from the council.

Happy and excited, I hurried to the town hall with the voucher in my pocket. From room to room, office to office, no one could honour nor understand the voucher. Still daylight, I rushed back to the forest with extreme anger and frustration. To my chagrin, the area was cleared and there was no one around. I began to pull up the trees that I had planted.

I joined Tahar and Mr Ali and wrote a poem:

> *Those men are big and tall*
> *Yet lie around all day long.*
> *They eat cold food with no mind,*
> *And in their empty hearts*
> *There is no song.*

I opened my heart to Tahar. 'You must help me buy a tent,' I told him.

'A tent? In a cold, rainy and damp land?'

'Yes,' I answered.

I asked him unrelentingly, and reluctantly, he succumbed. Tahar had a girlfriend. She was a prostitute, but they were very close and saw each other two or three times a week. They often went out, and Italy was their favourite holiday spot. She was well-connected and knew many black and white American soldiers in the city.

Frankfurt was like Melilla. Nothing was out of reach if the money was on the table, from drugs to guns and much more.

On Wednesday, we went to a chic restaurant in the middle of the town. Tahar ordered a beer; I asked for hot milk. While we were talking, a young blonde German woman arrived. She looked tall, extremely beautiful and polite. He stood up and they hugged each other. I wasn't expecting that.

'This is Monica,' he told me.

She sat beside him and asked me questions. Tahar did the translation. I felt she took an interest in me, but she was probably just being polite. I wasn't left out.

We ordered fried chicken with chips. I opted for another glass of milk, and they chose mocha coffee.

'Are you interested in a tent?' she asked me.

Tahar had obviously told her.

'Yes,' I said.

'I will find one for you,' she said with a smile, nodding.

The money I had borrowed from Tahar dwindled very fast from train tickets, city trams, food and hiding in cafes to escape the cold and seek warmth. I found a job in a restaurant from 8 p.m. until 2 a.m. – an inconvenient time. Unhappy, Mr Ali asked me to leave.

Proud and hurt, I grabbed my belongings and stuffed them in a bag. As I opened the door, Tahar arrived.

'I found a room,' I told him.

'What about the tent?' he asked. 'Monica might have found one.'

'Has she?'

'I haven't seen her yet,' he said.

'I am ready for the tent whenever she finds one,' I responded.

I caught the commuter train and headed to the central Frankfurt station. *I saved Ali's son's life and I curled up, like a dog in a corner, and that was too much for Mr Ali,* I thought to myself.

Thinking the love of Jesus was abundant, I headed to a gigantic, beautiful church a few yards from the Frankfurt river. I knocked. A priest, subdued and bored, opened the door. He looked absent and lifeless.

'I'm desperate for a room for a few days,' I told him.

With no expression, he gazed past me and slammed the door. I went back to the train station and thought it might be my home that night. It was busy with foreigners both strolling and racing past. I spied a small kiosk with a sign advertising rooms for rent. The prices were tailored for the well-off and wealthy.

'*L'oberge de la jeunesse*?' I asked the kiosk assistant sitting on a high chair in a cell-like room.

Graciously, he handed me the address and the tram number. I put my faith in him and hopped on the tram. The hostel sat on a small hill and was managed by an ex-soldier, tall and fat, who gave the impression of having an unrefined education. Vulgar words flew constantly out of both sides of his mouth, even when not needed.

Heaven was present. I rented a bunk bed in a room with three boys, one Turkish, one Irish and the other who liked to remain mysterious, changing name and country to suit his mood and the ambiance. To be safe in this place, one had to keep quiet, reserved and give the impression of being dangerous so no one would mess with him. Living by this rule, one ended up safe, but aloof and lonely. Though the hostel was full of people of different ages and from different cultures, each one flagged his personal problem, the family from where he came and the country he either loved or hated.

I befriended the Irish man, either in his late twenties or early thirties. He was tall, had a ruddy complexion and crackly voice. He came from Dublin, spoke German and a bit of French. We often met in the television room and spoke about politics, mainly against Americans, their support for dictators and Franco. I loaned him a few deutschmarks, but he never honoured the goodwill. As he worked in an office and was full of charm and twists, he slept with a new woman every week. I wondered where he found them all, but he had the gift of the gab and a deceiving charm. He used the women's toilet as a flophouse and put 'Out of Order' on the door. Despite it all, I liked talking to him, though truth and lies came simultaneously out of his mouth.

Days passed so quickly, I lost count, but my borrowed money shrank to almost zero. I spent hours and hours running from shop to shop, restaurant to restaurant, seeking a menial job. I ended up in a big restaurant on the main street where I worked from 4 p.m. to 2 a.m. I fried potatoes, cleaned toilets, washed dishes and mopped the floor. I was wrong when I thought I could nibble from my cooking.

'Stop! Stop!' shouted the manager. 'You have to pay for that!'

He was a Jew, and I thought he knew the Bible where it said, 'You should not muzzle the ox', but the worst was still waiting. The minimum wage was four deutschmarks. He paid me 2.15 per hour.

I am in the wrong place and in the wrong hand, I realised. *I'm not able to live, let alone be self-funding to go to the university.*

I thought about trading in spices, realising how expensive they were in Germany and how cheap in Morocco. With the idea in my mind and emotion simmering, I headed to see Tahar for an additional loan.

I boarded the train on Monday, his day off. The sky was broken, and the train wet. People's faces emitted Monday depression. Peering out, I saw the land like a carpet, pulled out from under my feet. Luckily, I caught Tahar. He was showering himself with perfume from neck to toes to meet Monica.

'Have you any idea about the tent?' I asked.

'Monica is very busy. We're going to get married.'

'Married?' I exclaimed. 'Are you not really Moroccan? She's not a virgin. She's a prostitute, and you are marrying her? Zolika is in Zaio.'

'She was not a virgin when I married her, and I support her,' he told me.

'Let me know when you're getting married,' I told him. 'I have a project, and I want you to lend me some money.'

'To do what?'

'Trade in spices, especially cumin,' I said.

'Where are you going to get them?'

'From Nador.'

'Yes, we grew cumin there. How much do you need?'

'One thousand deutschmarks.'

Tahar was peculiar and unique. He opened a case and showed me hundreds of pieces of Moroccan jewellery of all shapes, colours and sizes. It was enough to open a kiosk.

'Do you sell this jewellery?' I asked.

'No, I give them free.'

'Free? Why?'

'It cheers me to see German girls smiling. Where I work, they always have their lips zipped, except in those moments of wrath.'

'Does women's wrath frighten you?' I asked.

'Absolutely!'

'Now you have Monica on your back. Can I buy your jewellery?'

'Yes,' he said, nodding.

With Monica around, his jewellery had lost its magic. I borrowed five hundred deutschmarks in cash and the rest was the entire collection of jewellery. Leaving his hut, I was two thousand five hundred in debt, with no idea how to pay it back.

Tahar and I headed back to Frankfurt train station. He went to meet Monica, and I was looking for a spot to set up trading.

During the night, I tried to sell some jewellery to David, the Irish boy in the next bunk. I thought he might buy some to add to his trap and charm. He showed no interest.

'My ladies are not bohemian. They love Guinness,' he told me. David knew how to save money, just as he knew how to trap girls. We lunched at the university though neither of us was eligible. A swarm of students and academics poured into the refectory. Rice and beef casserole were popular. I couldn't find a much better place to sell my jewellery.

On a smart, colourful oriental rug just in front of the refectory, I spread my wares. Girls and boys besieged the rug. Bombarded with questions, I could only say '*Jawohl.*' Some women with pretty, but chubby, fingers were frustrated. The rings were too small. I didn't want to bring all my jewellery, as I was afraid the police might confiscate my goods and bankrupt me. Day after day, I became more familiar. Students began to talk to me, but didn't know what to make of me. For a few hours, I was a trader, and later, inside the refectory, I appeared as one of them.

Once, I shared a table with a professor. He was curious, and so was I. When he found I had come from Africa, Morocco, he poured his view on me.

'Africa is full of lazy people,' he told me. 'Even when they come and finish their studies, they go back, not to work like engineers but as politicians.' He referred to students he had known.

'It's not because they have a degree that they will go and build bridges,' I told him.

'Why not?' he said sharply.

'Such a project needs more than two graduated students. It needs the entire support of the government, the engineers, architects, builders . . .'

He left in a huff.

While I was standing outside selling my junk jewellery, three students came and stood to watch me. 'Are you Moroccan?' one asked.

'Yes.'

'We are as well.'

They looked to me to be too old to be students. I packed up my jewellery, and we went inside the refectory. They had left Morocco long ago, were all married to German women and had lost contact with their native land, but not their nostalgia.

As the time went on, I got to know Driss. He was studying economics. 'Can I borrow your identity?' I asked him once.

'Why?' he asked.

'So I can get a job.'

'Tricky one,' he said.

A few days later, still trading, I asked him the same question. I had won his trust. 'AEG is advertising jobs for students in its new division,' Driss told me.

'Can I borrow your papers?' I asked him.

9

AEG was a giant electronic company. It had a huge office in the centre of the city, not far from the river. There was also an offshoot branch on a hillside on the outskirts of the city, not far away from the tower with the revolving restaurant at the top. The offshoot itself contained two buildings with a distance between them. Dozens of engineers, designers and artists worked there. The company needed young, energetic, clever people to liaise among the three offices. It paid four marks per hour, but many people had left for different reasons.

Nervous, I prepared myself. I took Driss's identity paper and put my picture on it. Prepared to be sacked on the spot, I took tram number eleven and headed to the hillside. When I arrived at 7 a.m., the door was open. Mustering up courage, I knocked on the main door.

'*Bitte schon,*' I heard.

As I opened the door, I came face-to-face with a massive woman. She looked beautiful and sexy with few clothes on her shoulders, but her clothes and jewellery were expensive. Her room smelled of coffee and irresistible perfume.

Miraculously, she hired me, and I found her like a tyrant, taking and giving orders, running from her office to her boss.

She twittered around from her office to others'. She spied on everybody and was nosy and touchy. She knew everybody's date of birth and no one missed a birthday card, but she was at war with another woman, a secretary, just as important as herself but maybe not quite. The peace was the distance between them, but the telephone often broke the truce.

Carrying letters and documents, I shuttled among three buildings: the main one in the town and the two buildings of the offshoot branch. Taking the bus was awkward and subject to delay, but I always had to account for the time. As the time went by, I began to carry money. It was not in the quantity of a million, but it was tempting to run away from those ladies.

The relationship between Mrs Hermann and Mrs Schneider was acrimonious. I heard them shouting at each other and using vulgar words, like 'shit'. I saw Mrs Hermann put the telephone down and plunge into tears. When I wondered why she was crying, she told me it was because of Mrs Schneider.

'She isn't good,' she said. 'If she were, she wouldn't be divorced.'

I also heard Mrs Schneider accuse Mrs Hermann of being a sex toy. I saw them peering over each other's desks whenever they had the chance. They accidentally met once in the canteen while I was having my break. They were both cold, tense and nervous.

'You haven't brought the cup back,' said Mrs Hermann.

'Have you paid for them?' asked Mrs Schneider.

They squared up to each other. Suddenly, Mrs Schneider stretched out her big arm and ripped Mrs Hermann's clothes.

Pushing her back, Mrs Hermann grabbed Mrs Schneider's necklace and pulled her like an animal on a leash.

I was terrified. I came between them, but my size was no match for the two big German women. I was, however, able to startle them, and they quickly stopped. Mrs Hermann disappeared from the office and showed up later in the afternoon with new clothes. I didn't see Mrs Schneider until the following day. As recognition, she invited me to her room, where I had a lunch with her and her daughter. Both were sympathetic to me. They gave me a job even when it wasn't needed, as I was paid by the hour.

In the main mail room where we sat and talked, I met a Frenchman who had been a prisoner of war for many years in Germany. Freed, he had never gone back to his native land. Beside him sat a Jewish man who had been bankrupted by the Nazis.

'They took everything I had,' he told me.

'No compensation?' I asked him.

'How can you compensate for the loss of life?' he asked.

To add to his bankruptcy, he had a boy lover who took every penny he earned.

'I am just mad,' he told me when I refused to lend him money.

10

Living in a hostel was like living in a mental hospital. Noise and fights filled the nights. Thefts were commonplace. It was either money, toothpaste, toothbrushes, shampoo or combs. No one could own an umbrella for more than a week. Things flew at night.

As I began to make some money, paid weekly cash in hand, I was determined to use the bank, but that didn't save me.

Coming back from work on payday, I hung my jacket above my bed and went to pee.

Returning to my room within a few minutes, I found my wallet had been fleeced. Outraged, I flew out to the corridor to look for a thief and a fight, but found no one. The hall was empty, calm, with doors locked, all in peace but me. Had I met anyone, he would have been my primary suspect. I decided on that night to buy a tent to not be in the way of people and be close to nature. I took the commuter train and headed to see Tahar.

Tahar was a foodie. He possessed the art of the kitchen and a vast knowledge of Indian spices, from yellow colour to sweet. Black pepper, cumin and ginger were his fighting tools, and his hut was always filled with mixed aromas. A black cauldron from Morocco was simmering on a propane stove.

'What are you cooking tonight?' I asked him.

'Couscous,' he said.

His brother, he and I all sat around a small table brought from Morocco.

'Moroccan couscous in a foreign land,' his brother joked.

After couscous, we had green tea with mint. On night duty, his brother left, but before leaving, he ignited a fight.

'Tahar is mad,' he told me.

'No, if he were, he wouldn't be here. He would be in the hospital,' I said.

'Wait and see,' he said.

'I am going to get married to Monica, the prostitute. My brother hates me for that,' Tahar said. 'He would kill me if it didn't mean being locked out of paradise.'

'Maybe he's right,' I suggested.

'To kill me?' said Tahar.

'You know I don't mean that. Would you invite me to the wedding?' I asked, hoping to water down my gaffe.

'Would you like to be my best man?'

He surprised me. 'I would like to, but I'm foreign to the culture,' I said. When Tahar came back to normality and a good mood, I reminded him of my request to buy a tent.

'Why a tent?' he asked.

He had forgotten our conversation long ago in the restaurant.

'I'm living in a hell as described in the Koran. You keep burning for eternity and there's no way out of it,' I said. 'The hostel is noisy. My roommates are rough, dirty and untidy. The light is never switched off. I feel my head is like a rotten egg. A thief took my last wages, and in my own room.'

'Let's meet next week,' said Tahar.

He was a man of his word. After a week jostling between two secretaries and between AEG's main office and the new office, I met Tahar. Monica was with him.

'She is taking a week off,' he told me.

Is prostitution a job or a perversion? I asked myself. Neither of them took alcohol. We all drank coffee mocha. Surprise, surprise.

'We found a tent for you,' Tahar told me. 'Still interested?'

'Absolutely!' I began to complain about the hostel, and both shushed me. This moaning was a habit I had picked up from living with my sisters while I was a shepherd.

In Monica's car, we drove a few miles outside the town to see the tent. The owner was a strange, tattooed man, high and mighty, apparently living on his own in a caravan but encircled by a fierce pack of dogs. The look of him, especially his long, untidy beard, scared me.

'Where are you from?' he asked me.

'Morocco,' I replied.

'I lived in Morocco,' he said. 'In the north.'

'Why did you go there?' I asked him.

'To fuck and be fucked.'

It's you and people like you, I told myself, *who took sex to a holy land, distributed drugs and spread diseases among people whose lives depended simply on sardines and oranges. You came back to find a job and comfort, but none of that for those people left behind.*

The tent was old, but in good condition. He was happy to get rid of it, and I was delighted to grab it.

Buying a tent wasn't the end, though. Where to pitch it? 'Don't go near any pub,' advised Tahar. 'Hide or minimise your visibility. Drunks will attack you.'

This advice terrified me. I had seen what Friday and Saturday evenings did to people. Like snakes, they shed their humanity, giggled for no reason and talked with no listeners. Females tried to excite, and males tried to impress. It was a game. It was an art. Only the skilful ended with prey.

Taking Tahar's advice to the extreme, I made myself invisible. I avoided public areas and pubs. Drunken men terrified me.

Can anyone lose his mind and retrieve it? Never. They might turn into animals, I thought. *Seriously, can anyone come back to life from death? If it did happen, it would never be the same.*

Christian people drank wine to cement themselves with God. The best, I thought, was to drink coffee to be sober and alert. Terrified of being molested in my tent by those heavy, big and meaty German men, I isolated myself.

With Tahar's and Monica's help, I moved out of Frankfurt. I settled on a bus route to AEG. It was a beautiful spot dotted with trees. Among those living creatures, I pitched my tent, small but adequate. Having left the hostel, I settled like a hermit or a madman. My first night was a residence in heaven. There were no slamming doors or lights on and off.

As thanksgiving, I grabbed the soil and sprinkled it over my shoulders for being calm and receiving. I praised the sky for the dark night and for being a generous blanket.

I awakened fresh and feeling young again. *Where has my strength been?* I wondered. There was no water, and I had to adapt and train my bowel and bladder. Shaving wasn't a problem; I hardly had any hair, just tender and fresh cheeks. I went to work earlier than anyone, even the boss. I carried toothbrush, toothpaste and a comb and used AEG's facilities. As the company paid for lunch for its staff, that was all I needed for the day.

I lived in peace for several months. I was afraid of no one, but many were of me. As it was a beautiful spot, people brought their dogs and wandered. I could peer at them from my tent, but whenever I came out, they ran away. I knew I wasn't mad or even deranged, just unlucky.

Now and again, I met Tahar, always at the train station café. We talked about politics, but never religion. I knew he was in love with Monica, but I was surprised when he handed me an invitation to his wedding. *Having sex with a German woman might be great*, I thought, *but to marry Monica!*

I had never been at a European wedding, had no clue of what to wear, what type of gift to offer, or what the right words were to say. All I knew was that Tahar already had a wife in Zaio.

To make myself smart, I bought new trousers and a jacket. I walked for hours and hours to find the church. It was gigantic. History was talking. The organist, in a secluded area, hammered a pipe organ, and it hit me as though he were announcing Armageddon.

I was seated by a young woman who gave me a generous smile that disturbed me the whole night. If I could have found her after the wedding, I would have tried to get another smile.

I had no clue what the priest said, but I heard the word 'love' used several times. I concluded that he meant love was the basis of Tahar's and Monica's marriage, not the law. That

Tahar was already married wasn't an issue. On this basis, same-sex marriage was just as good as the heterosexual one. When Tahar and Monica left the church to go on their honeymoon in Tuscany, I went back to my tent.

Living there provided me with peace, tranquillity and money-saving, but my job was not great or appreciated. I felt despised and made to feel the lowest of the low.

When the summer came to its end, Louvain University confirmed my place to study medicine. I put my tent up for sale and went to a posh restaurant to retrieve my ego. It was here where AEG staff took their wives and brought their girlfriends.

Accidentally, for the lack of tables, I was seated with a French girl working as an au pair. She was stunningly beautiful, well-dressed and polite. We spoke French and stayed late. It just happened that a group of AEG staff had come for a dinner and saw us. Impressed by the French girl, they kept watching me.

Coming back Monday to work, I found news and rumours that Jusef had a beautiful girlfriend. Mr Miller, who had once sacked me, asked me where I had met this stunning girl. I was not ready for the truth.

'In Frankfurt,' I told him.

'Is she your girlfriend?' he asked.

'You saw for yourself!' I told him.

11

Louvain. Here I am. Out of the train, I joined an army of ants. They knew where to go, but I didn't. The city was Flemish, dotted with Walloons. It had a sad history, twice destroyed by Germany, but had sprung again from the ashes. It spoke history and exhibited beauty. Buildings, streets, churches, cafés, bars, open markets. However, Louvain was not Frankfurt, just as Frankfurt was not Morocco. It was dynamic, yet calm and subdued. It could be even depressing and lonely.

University Catholic du Louvain was nestled in this historic and cultural city. In the late sixties, the university was forced to roost somewhere else in the Walloon area and took the name Louvain La Neuve. It was a political cleansing some thought to be suicidal; others cheered the move. I was caught in this transitional time.

Arriving in the afternoon, I didn't know which direction to take or where to spend the night. Hotels were few. Bed and breakfasts didn't exist either. Following the crowd, I headed down the main street toward the city hall and came to another street where I saw a small hotel. A huge woman was sitting in an armchair in the front room and peering out.

'Do you have a room?' I asked in French, stepping in.

'Yes,' she answered. 'Wait,' she added.

Another woman appeared, a younger version of the first, extremely broad and stealing many facial traits from the first. *Her daughter*, I assumed, *more agile*. While waiting, I noticed an English-speaking female arrive. She was looking for accommodation, too.

The landlady, not knowing we were unrelated, lumped us together and took us to a room. The room was modest, had no private facilities, but a big chamber pot with a pitcher of water.

'This is a lovely bed, and it's big enough for you two,' she said.

The English woman went berserk. 'He is not my friend!' she shouted.

Hearing her shouting, the old woman screamed back, 'Here we are international!' She made things worse.

'I'm not sleeping with him!' the woman shrieked. 'I am not international!'

Paying up front, I took the room and went to sleep straightaway. The English woman took another room.

I slept in and the lady awakened me as I had requested. It was breakfast time. The sun was bright and shiny, but the air was mixed with a cold breeze. The dining room was small, dotted with a few tables. A strong, excellent coffee was hard to resist. The aroma filled my nostrils. I was first in the room and only one large table was laid. I sat down and began buttering a slice of pain de campagne. The young lady, the daughter, with a smile and new clothes, brought me coffee and hot milk.

The English woman stepped into the dining room. The daughter smiled and said, '*Pour le table avec son monsieur.*'

Looking unhappy, the English woman looked around. No other table was laid, and she muttered, 'I want a table on my own.'

The mother heard her, and both rushed to lay the table for her with butter, jam, bread, hot milk and coffee.

Leaving the dining room and coming to the front room, I was stopped by both ladies who said, '*Cette femme est quelque chose!*' with a broad Flemish accent. They either felt embarrassed or sorry for me.

* * *

TO GET INTO UCL HAD been difficult, but to come out with some relevant qualifications was even more so. Double registrations, university and police created problems. The admissions department was big and crowded with Flemish speakers. Following the queue bit by bit, I reached the desk, efficiently run by a big man in his late thirties. He was the processor. I handed him the university's offer, Science Naturelle.

He looked at it and said, 'Financial proof.'

'What?'

'Either a grant or a bank statement that you have enough money.'

I didn't have either.

I had put my money in the Societe General. I rushed to the bank and brought a bank statement. Going back to the processor, I handed him my bank paper.

He was furious. 'That is not enough!' he shouted. 'Do you know that you are in Belgium?' The day was dark. I left the office, wondering. Cloud over cloud. I had only my shoulders and my legs to rely upon. Rushing to the little hotel, I asked if I could stay for a few more days. Mother and daughter looked delighted with the prospect of more income from someone who had none.

On my third day, I went to the bank and transferred everything to another bank just a few metres away. As soon as my money registered at the new bank, I asked for a bank statement. With two bank statements in my hand, I headed to the admissions office. I handed the processor the two statements from different banks and with different amounts. He looked at them and nodded, satisfied. Registered with the university, now I had to register with the police.

The university offered no accommodation, but had a service that contained a list of all private landlords renting rooms. The hunt started. It was a matter of who you were, distance and price. Systematically, I went through the list, but in addition, most owners advertised their rooms above their windows. I knocked on many doors and for several days. It was worse than Frankfurt. Some owners, mostly women, refused to come to the door if they saw who was knocking. Some opened the door and told lies. 'It's already reserved.'

Others were bold and honest. 'I don't take foreigners,' one woman told me. 'Foreigners don't go home on weekends and at Christmas. I take only Belgians and from Luxemburg. I want the weekends free, just to myself, my daughter and her husband.'

Other owners bordered on racism. 'I want just Walloons, not even Flemish,' one told me. 'Walloons are well-educated, mannered and wealthy.'

I ventured out from the centre of town and dug into my pocket – twice the price of the ordinary room. The landlords were harsh and aggressive.

'No visitors, boys or girls. Never be out later than 9 p.m.; the door is latched. No cooking in the room, but you are allowed to smoke. Never enter the lounge or the kitchen.'

Despite the restrictions, I was happy to get a place. The room was clean, sun-facing and at the back. The kitchen, directly below the room, was always busy and smelling of food. It was noisy with talking and giggling, and the wafting of evaporating beer drifted up toward me. The family seemed happy.

On one occasion, however, I heard furniture cracking. Shouts and yells followed, but no police were called. It was a real family brawl.

The lady later came and apologised. 'My daughter tried to strangle her little sister,' she said.

The university was scattered all over the town. The faculty of medicine was even worse. A poor timetable and organisation, with courses borrowed from other departments, meant a huge distance between classes, and my not having any means of transport paralysed me. To add to that, I was short of money and jobs were scarce.

Philosophy and science attracted me. I liked the logic, the formal logic, cosmology, epistemology and phenomenology, but I was not one among equals. Belgians were rich. Most of them had a car and spent weekends at home, leaving nothing to be desired. I found myself surrounded by Swiss students from the German region. They were well-fed and well-clothed. Once I asked a boy, sitting beside me, what his father did.

'He's a bank manager,' he answered.

I asked another one.

'My father is a dentist,' he replied.

In the same class, there were many Americans and Canadians. Most of them had been forced to do a one-year course before being allowed to do a PhD.

* * *

SURPRISE, SURPRISE! I FAILED IN June and had to resit. *What have I done wrong?* I wondered. I asked Professor Van Stan Bergan to have a mock exam. I spent the entire morning answering his questions in writing. I handed him my paper and had to wait until the following week for feedback.

When I saw him in the lecture room, he was abrupt, arrogant and frank. 'You are intelligent,' he told me, 'but take note. We are not French, Arabs or novelists. We are scientists in whatever we do. Precision and rigour is our method. French lack precision. Arabs, I don't know.' He nodded his head. 'If you aren't precise, we would never know if you have understood. *Presizez, presizez, dit le maitre.* Goodbye.'

I wasn't in a glorious position to argue with him. I had failed my exams. Before starting revision, I needed a job. One was advertised in the forest, a few miles away from the town. A Coca-Cola director and a surgeon lived in a semi-isolated and secluded field and needed a path from their houses to the main road. To reach the grove, I borrowed an old bicycle from a friend. The Coca-Cola director's wife was in charge. She was wearing a pair of open pyjamas when I arrived just after ten in the morning and was surrounded by cheeky, unruly children.

Pleading and begging them with a pathetic voice, she seemed to have no authority over them. She didn't know who might turn up for the job. Sadly, it was me.

She provided me with a pickaxe, shovel, iron brush and a wheelbarrow. Her children, she and I all descended from her hillside house to the main road. Digging, clearing, and levelling was the job. Pretty tough for someone hungry.

During my labour, her teenage children kept bursting out of the house to check on me, one after another. Time and time again. They took pleasure observing me via binoculars. While working, I was offered no water, let alone food. Both the surgeon and the director went in and out, but never stopped or said 'hello' as they passed.

The job took three hours. When I finished, I went to the lady to collect my pay. She didn't have enough money and roamed from room to room shouting and gathering coins. She came with a large bucket full of Belgian coins. Nervously, she sat down and began counting over the huge kitchen table. She kept losing count and restarted again and again. Not sure of the figure, she asked her children to count. A fight started immediately among them. She chased them and asked me to come the following day.

'No, ma'am,' I said. 'I will not have a bicycle and I have another job moving furniture.' Just then, at three o'clock, her husband arrived. Eyes behind tinted glasses, a pipe stuck between his jaws, he looked at the money on the table.

'Do you have money to pay *ce monsieur*?' she asked.

'I didn't come from the bank,' he replied.

Gazing at the coins covering the table, he sat to count. Just like his wife, he lost track. 'You have almost enough here,' he told his wife. 'Short only one hundred nineteen francs.' To make up for the shortage, he asked me, 'How many breaks did you take?'

'Not even one,' I replied.

'Come next week,' he added with a dismissive tone, handing me the bucket.

One my way home, I got wet. A torrential rain hit the ground, and my bicycle began to lose its chain.

Now, furniture. I had had many jobs in my life, but this was the worst of them all. Either the housebuilder or the furniture manufacturer had got it wrong. We had to move furniture in and out through the window, as the front door was too narrow. Having neither the stamina nor the muscle for the job, I quit. It was also time to revise.

Rigour and precision were in my mind. I mustn't be either French or Arab. Cliché. The French referred to Belgians as idiots, and Belgians retorted that a Frenchman is a man of nonsense. Clichés didn't always help, but rigour and precision did, with considerable damage.

With precision, rigour, exactitude, I lost my taste for literature, novels and poetry, which I had enjoyed enormously. No matter how, precision could never stop the ambiguity of language. Lawyers would always resort to interpretation and reinterpretation. Theologians were the victims of their own language. In this sense, Wittgenstein and his followers had failed. We lived in a world of interpretation. That didn't mean, however, that precision had to be abandoned or that we lived in a nonsensical world.

12

I had taken advice and moved on successfully. I got out of my isolation and made friends. Professor Dop, a lawyer, had become a logician. Formal logic was his toy of choice. Dirty, always smoking and laughing, he was a man to reckon with. In his lecture, I came across four young, talented Jesuits, all smart and in uniform. They puzzled me. How could someone who lived illogically study logic?

As time went on, I befriended them. They were good people and also do-gooders, activists and present in any conference, be it political, theological or just intellectual. Men of culture. They were not alone. Well-educated nuns were the same. Talks on the Vietnam War, faith and sex were the topics of choice. I didn't have the luxury of enough time to join each talk. Juggling my jobs and studies kept my hands full.

A well-advertised talk by an imminent scholar from Brussels was organised. As I had a free evening, I joined the club. The title was 'The Job of Holy'. I thought it was about an electronic device. Professor Ladiere was teaching us cosmology, something orbiting around the earth, I thought. I arrived a bit late, and the talk was informal. A handsome man in his forties with a church uniform was surrounded by beautiful women, just like a pharaoh, the King of Egypt. As he spoke and opened his mouth, his teeth shone like stars, full of gold. He talked of the cosmos between the Holy Spirit and the scripture. Then I realised it was not about an electronic device, but about something more cynical.

As the talk progressed, the word 'trinity' came out of his mouth more and more often. I wondered what was wrong with those people? I put my hand up to ask him a question.

'Where did you get this construction? Who are the builder and the architect for it?' I asked. 'You can't build an edifice and then start to make it God.'

He paused and looked puzzled. Suddenly, the audience turned against me. 'You don't understand! You don't understand!' men and women shouted at me from every direction.

I felt like a dog in the midst of wolves.

Then, coffee time. A young, happy-looking woman arose, walked around, spoke to the speaker and her friends, then handed me a coffee as she sat beside me. Looking at her, I was reminded of Khadija with an oval face and dimpled cheeks, a thousand miles away. She had an extremely attractive smile.

'You didn't understand the speaker,' she told me, repeating the chorus.

That put me immediately on offence and defence. I was allergic to the phrase, 'didn't understand.' It reminded me of maths class. 'You don't understand,' he used to tell us, each time we were stuck. As a class, we assumed we were stupid. That night, the entire pack of wolves resuscitated the past and accused me of being thick. I might well have been so. I wasn't expecting the audience to turn into a pack. I had enough issues.

My conversation with this attractive woman, Connie, wasn't sweet. We went in different directions.

'What do you do?' I asked her.

'I'm a nun,' she replied.

'A nun with no uniform?'

'Nuns have to live with the times.'

'Where do you live?' I asked, as I had some doubt she was a nun.

'In a convent,' she replied.

Louvain or Leuven: if you were a dreamer, this was the place; if you were an activist, politician, this was the bastion; but if you wanted to hibernate in reading, there were plenty of books. If you wanted to work and study, you had to seek and knock. There was no substitute for stamina and hard work. Leuven was also a lonely planet; the society was family oriented, introverted. Being a foreign student wasn't the best attraction for local people, intensely focused and pragmatic. Being Moroccan and Muslim (no alcohol or bars) sealed my fate.

There were many, many Latinos from South America. They stuck to each other. They grouped and glued like wasps, speaking exclusively Spanish. Some even took notes in Spanish. *Powerful minds*, I thought, *to instantly convert French to Spanish.*

Searching for jobs, I met George, an American from the Midwest. Like many Americans, he was on a special programme. Later, I met him in Ms Mansion's class. An expert in Greek, she taught the Aristotle metaphysic. She was rigorous in thinking and cruel in marking. George did not fit in. He was big, relaxed and lax. He loved coffee, cigarettes and talking and spent all his nights writing poetry. As he couldn't get up in the early morning, he missed the Aristotle metaphysic, a notoriously complicated subject made more so by the teaching of Ms Mansion.

Throughout the year, he came to visit me and borrow my notes. Though I liked his visits, he choked me with smoke. Sometimes he accused me of not knowing how to take notes, as they didn't make sense for him, being either too much or too little.

'Get up, come to the lecture and take notes for yourself!' I replied, but this was not an option for him.

He loved America. I never heard him criticising or moaning about it. As I hadn't seen him for a few days, I went to check on him. I found him standing at the window smoking cigarettes and peering out at the traffic. He looked preoccupied, sad and depressed. *Something is wrong*, I thought.

As we sat drinking coffee, he burst out, 'I am called.'

'To do what?' I asked.

'Vietnam,' he answered.

That didn't mean too much for me. It was all far away. He invited me to visit the Midwest, his hometown of Quincy, and invited me to stay with his parents and find a job in the United States.

'The land of chosen people,' he said, jokingly.

'I wouldn't go to America unless I am married to an American woman,' I said.

'Why American?' he asked.

'They are fatty and meaty.'

'They will sit on you!'

'That's what I want!' I answered, laughing.

Time passed too quickly. He packed his notes, books, intending to come back to do his PhD. The day before he left from the Zaventem airport to fly to the United States, he came to see me at Ravan Street. He reiterated his invitation.

'I will still be here when you come back,' I told him.

I didn't expect to hear from him. I was self-funding and had no time to dream, socialise, or even culture my mind with current events.

A few months later, I received a white letter stamped 'Airmail' from the United States. I jumped to read it, wondering what was inside. I carefully tore the envelope, trying not to damage the return address. First, I noticed the writing was different from anything I knew. I kept reading as quickly as possible, intending to read it deeply again.

Dear Joseph,

George has spoken of you many times, at each meal, mentioning how much he enjoyed your friendship and how kind you were to him, lending him your notes and supplying him with coffee. He wants us to invite you to Quincy. With our hearts shattered and broken, I want to let you know that George was killed in Vietnam on his first day of action. The helicopter in which he was being transported was downed. We would like to see you and hear anyone talking about George.

George's Mother, Judy

George's death made a crack in my emotions. It was too soon, too quick and too brutal. It opened a third eye in my perception. There were many discussions, talks and conferences about Vietnam, and I went to many of them. Trying to fathom why Americans travelled that far to die and kill was like getting into a cellar with no light. True to the nature of the beast, students were anti-war and so were most of academia. A professor from the University of Montreal, Canada, gave us a talk. He blamed Henry Kissinger for many of the atrocities because the Americans increased air bombardment in the hope discussions might go his way, but did they?

13

I was in my fourth year of university. It was the summer holidays, and, completing my thesis, I was spending a lot of time in the main library. As I was leaving the library, someone ambushed me. Familiar and unfamiliar.

'Joseph!' he shouted.

Nothing rang a bell. Suddenly, from the present, I moved to the past. Robert had been my classmate in Logic and was an ordained priest. He was in lay clothes, not as I remembered him, and a woman, double his age, stood nearby waiting and watching.

'Coffee?' he asked.

We left the library, crossed the street and went to a corner coffee bar. His wife ordered a coffee, but he preferred beer.

'I am fasting,' I told him. 'It's Ramadan.'

'You might be wondering,' he said. 'I tore up my vow and married this beautiful woman.'

I didn't think she was beautiful myself. She had a round face, a piggy nose and literally no neck. She took no part in the conversation except to watch Robert as if he were a stray child.

'Are you Christian?' I asked him, joking.

'I don't know.'

'A believer, certainly?'

'Not in God. You cannot explain the unknown with the unknown.'

It took me time to fathom this statement and to catch up with him.

'It's all an uncontrolled volcano. It spews its smoke, ashes and gases into the sky, then all meet in clouds, rain, wind and fall down. You can't explain the unknown with the unknown,' he explained.

Robert had certainly had time to meditate.

'What are you doing now?' I asked.

'Finishing a diploma to teach religious studies,' he answered.

Robert, Daniel, Jack and Paul had all been very close friends and happy people exploring logic. They were also all priests, but I hadn't seen any of them for over two years.

'Jack is going to be married,' he told me. 'He's teaching Latin in a private school. Paul is already married and working in the foreign office.'

'What about Daniel?' I asked him.

'We don't speak to him, even if we meet in the street.'

'Why have you all deserted the church and broken your vows? Error of youth or rejection of faith?' I asked.

Robert paused for a while. Both his wife and I expected an answer. 'Faith and the church. The church, as a core, is afraid of changes. Modern times are challenging.'

'Afraid of hippyism? Feminism? Communism?' I asked.

'Fear of everything.'

I knew Robert. He had not gotten on with the hierarchy of the church. He gave them a hard time. He wanted to be a revolutionary and turn the church upside-down. He refused to be reined in.

'Change in the church and in faith is dangerous,' I said.

His wife looked at me and agreed, for the first time.

'Would you be happy to sack the pope?' I asked. 'Would you be happy to sack the cardinals? Would you be happy to change the mass?'

'If you do that, you will be left with nothing, I suppose,' he said. 'Change is a change.'

'Should the change come from the top or the bottom?' I asked.

'From the bottom.'

'Then the church would turn into a communist party,' I told him. 'The divine would be interred. That might even lead to regional theology.'

'The top should listen.'

'Then you want to turn the top into scribes.'

'Scribes are a problem,' he said.

'Then scribes would be to faith what artists are to art,' I said. 'I don't need to admire or sanctify Picasso to enjoy or even identify myself with his art. I don't need to go through all that he did to taste love or understand sex. It just happened to be he who painted "Les Demoiselles d'Avignon". Faith and clergy are not one. I don't need to cut my ear off like van Gogh to understand the sorrow in man. I don't need to get married and divorced five times like the Egyptian Hada-Sultan to understand marriage and divorce. Faith and church, like art and artist, don't need to be one, though a good understanding between them is vital.'

'Religion as the church is not democratic,' he said.

'But faith is,' I added.

14

When I saw a picture of the Sistine Chapel, I realised what Michelangelo meant and believed: the agony of God and man. God reached his right hand as far as he could; Adam stretched his left arm and index finger, both attempting to meet and both failing. Adam couldn't reach God and God couldn't save Adam. Will and temptation were exercised from both sides, yet the distance remained. God's hand and man's hand were left strenuously dangling in the air and hope. The fosse was small, but still it was a fosse. The fosse existed not because of original sin, but because of man's sorrow. The fosse was filled with tears and pain. This was not a good position for either. Man retreated, but, in his loneliness and hopelessness, resorted to blaming God, making judgments and complaining. By doing so, the fosse got bigger and bigger, leaving God in the dock.

15

Sexuality was the oxygen of the late sixties and early seventies. Freud had impregnated the air and few people could remain unaffected by it. It was all in the hand of a pioneer, and it might be still. Professor Dewealheus, a star among psychiatrists, charged me to do some research on sexuality. The written literature was either scarce or vulgar.

A massive conference called 'Sexuality' was advertised, and the speaker was a respectable, famous doctor. The conference was in a cinema. The theatre was packed with young and old people, singles and couples. The speaker brought out two actors and demonstrated sexual positions.

As I was sitting, suddenly a young lady sat beside me. The demonstration was extremely embarrassing and provocative. I sat still, but from time to time, glanced at the woman on my right. I thought she recognised me, as she kept her face turned away from me. Then, a flash from the past came. *This is Connie, the nun I argued with!*

To add to the embarrassment, I said, 'Are you Connie, the nun?'

'Yes,' she said, looking extremely intimidated.

This is not a place for her, I thought.

'Jusef,' she said. 'How are you doing?'

'I am doing some research.'

'I still remember you. You often come into my mind.'

'You did want to convert me to Christianity, didn't you?'

When the conference ended, she invited me for a coffee just a few metres away from the cinema. She was so beautiful, but somehow distant. I wondered what had called her to be a nun and what had caused her to be uncovered. How was she able to combine two worlds into one? Coming from a country where everybody is suspicious of everyone and everything, I wondered if she were not a spy. I had met this woman twice now: once in a theological talk and now in a sexual demonstration. *Who is she?* I wondered.

Talking to her, I was in two minds. She was all mind and no emotion. She brought the Vietnam War to the discussion, the bourgeois, American imperialism, Russian imperialism and Christianity.

'Not long ago, I lost a good friend,' I told her. 'Speaking of bourgeois, I am not one of them. I might not be the poorest in the university, but I am the poorest in my class. As religion goes, here I am. Christianity is the most bizarre religion on the planet!'

'Do you really think so?' she asked.

'Jesus, the son of no one. He was condemned, crucified and buried. Then he was dancing again. As if this were not mental enough, the Holy Spirit was added, standing on His feet and gazing at the sky. Then, to add to the collage, Jesus is God. This is no more than a rainbow of incoherent mosaic,' I told her.

She looked at me and cried. Tears cascaded and flooded her cheeks. I yanked a hanky out of my pocket and offered it to her, but she didn't move. So emotionally touched, I wiped her tears. *What soft skin,* I thought.

A pause.

She stretched out her hand to me, and I put mine in hers.

'I'm originally from Fresno, California. I will be your friend, but on one condition: you are Christian.'

Holding her hand firmly, taking advantage of the closeness offered, with an overwhelming emotion, I told her, 'Connie, God is not a man, not a woman, not a child, not a tree, not a flower, not a hill. God was neither born nor gave birth. Not, not, not, not, not, not is His definition. Never is, never is, never is, never is, never is, is His best definition. I would like to tell you one secret of my life. As a boy, I was a shepherd. How God has created the universe and how the universe has come into being is puzzling me now just as it puzzled me when I was a shepherd scanning the stars.'

We left the table, and I kissed her on her cheek.

16

Caught between objectivity and obsession, I liked my little piece of work, my thesis, which finished my undergraduate degree. I discovered nothing, but I learned a lot. Getting a grant from the university to do a PhD was a revolution in my life. I had never had one before. Professor Dewealheus was the top Belgian phenomenologist of his time. He loved research and writing, but had very little contact with students. He didn't accept students easily, and most shied away from him. He gained a reputation as a difficult man with whom to work.

All meetings were at his home, a terraced building looking at the park, close to the newsstand and Alma II, the biggest university restaurant. I liked his succinct and cryptic style. Forcing myself, I took a risk and phoned him at home. To my surprise, he answered politely and gave me an appointment in six weeks' time.

I knew I must be on time, not one minute late or early. I went to his house, waited outside and watched the time ticking. It was a big three-storey house with a large, impressive library on the first floor. Facing the view toward the park, he sat down at his majestic desk, and I sat on a sofa far away. Due to his arthritis, he looked crooked in his chair. It was apparent when he walked.

I didn't know how and why he launched on Sartre. 'He wrote fast and very richly compared to many writers of his genre. Sartre is communist, defending the working class, but France has a class below the working class, the peasants.'

I had seen the hard life of French peasants myself, but maybe Professor Dewealheus knew even more because his wife was French.

'Simone de Beauvoir,' he said, 'is a bitter woman.'

'As I have a good interest and background in science, I am thinking of continuity for my PhD,' I said.

He liked my background, but not the idea of neurology. At that time, phenomenology and psychiatry were obsessed with *l'inconscient* (the unconscious). No one liked what Freud had said, but no one had come with anything acceptable as a working alternative. Contradiction and accusation were in every corner.

'Would you like to tackle this topic, with all risks on your shoulders? If you succeed, I will support you to prolong your grant for another year to finish your research on sexuality,' he said.

I spent almost one and a half hours listening to him. The topic was extremely difficult and there was very little material with which to work. The few articles that had been written were immediately refuted. To this day, if one were to ask the top professor, 'what is *l'inconscient*?', one would get no clear answer. *L'inconscient* intertwined with consciousness made my life very difficult. I left and didn't see him until one year later.

Getting a grant for three years, I didn't need to spend hours and hours criss-crossing the town looking for menial jobs. I was called for a job many times but, once there, the job didn't exist. Residing in the libraries was a privilege, but cut off from reality, I knew. Not every restaurant, café or shop owner was a capitalist. I was a lodger in three different houses, and none had a telephone or a bath with a tub. To make a telephone call, I had to go to the station and join the queue.

I lived in C. Monier. My neighbour was an American professor at the university. Having a room at the back, my window looked directly into his back garden. Small, it had no trees or grass, and, overlooked by buildings, it was in the dark shadows day and night. A big pile of sand was plopped in the middle. It was his gym. He, his wife and beautiful daughter would go there and dig the sand as if they were under the order of the French legion d'honour. The sand could be dug three or four times a day. Whenever I felt bored or stupid, I stood up, went to the window and peered over the professor's garden, the only open space.

Out of the blue, I suddenly felt dizzy and nauseous. I didn't leave my room for several days. Suspicious, the landlady came to check. She found me in bed, a few books on the floor, stale coffee left in the cup. The room looked untidy, but not dirty.

'Are you okay?' she asked.

'Not really, madam.'

'What's wrong?'

'I feel dizzy whenever I stand and nauseous when I move.'

'You should go to the hospital, perhaps,' she said.

I had had many conversations with my landlady before. Her husband was clever, but an alcoholic. She often put ipecac in his drink to stop him. She knew a lot about the hospital because of her husband's condition. She shut the door and descended the stairs. I knew no one with a car to ask for a lift. Like a cloud moving in and out, my dizziness hit me and went. Determined to get over this malady, I took a taxi to the hospital.

Two young Flemish doctors took care of me and decided it was labyrinthitis.

'Given rest and time, the body will take care of itself and restore balance,' they told me.

Some doctors were more curious than others. These were exceptionally interested in Morocco for an adventurous holiday.

Leaving the clinic room and coming up to reception, packed with patients, I saw two middle-aged Moroccan men in their midst. More likely, they had heard us talking of Fes and Marrakesh. One of them stopped me.

It's hard to hide pain just as it's hard to share it, I thought, looking at one of them in severe pain, leaning his back against his hands.

'We're in the building trade,' one said.

After several weeks, my balance was restored and the joy of life was back. I loved cowboy films and wouldn't miss it if there were one in the town. I loved the heroism, roughness, toughness and the nonsense that went with it. On my way to see a film in the main street, I popped in to see the two Moroccan men.

Shock and surprise! There were ten men living in a completely dilapidated house with no gate and no door. Three of the four rooms had no roof and were falling down, as if an earthquake had shaken the house. The herd of men were all squashed into one single room and sleeping over each other, spread-eagled. There were no chairs or sofas, but a lot of food was scattered on the floor. They did the cooking in the next room when the weather allowed.

'Ten of you. Can you not rent a flat?' I asked.

'We can't. We're paid cash in hand; the builder moves us from one job to another in different locations. Sometimes just one of us, and sometimes more.'

I aborted my evening joy. I couldn't have enjoyed the film. I went straight back to my room and wondered, sadly, *Can humanity ever be different? Will humanity ever be one flesh, one colour? The colour doesn't matter. It can be red, blue, pink. If there were just one colour, no other colour could be put over it. If it were red, but red, red, red, and so red, then no blue or grey could be brushed over it. If it were blue, blue, blue, so blue, the red would spoil it. If it were all one flesh, well-made, intrinsically elaborate, painters would be dispossessed of colour and throw their brushes away. Political systems with all their colour, just like religions with all their promises, fail to give man one single colour, one humanity, to reduce the pain and inequality.*

17

As a child, I spoke exclusively Tarifit, a language spoken only in the north of Morocco. It mirrored the people, the land, the sun, the moon, the stars and the harsh life of the region. Like sea waves, its accent changed from tribe to tribe, village to village, town to town, region to region. The physiology and the nerves that rose up and down the throat told different stories. From Tamsman to Zaio, one had to listen carefully to understand.

When I revolted and adventured to Fes, I had to first learn the Moroccan dialect, then classic Arabic, and later, French. As if I were driving a truck and looking into the rear-view mirror, the distance got bigger and bigger. But no matter how big and deep a river was, it could never wipe clean the moss trapped deeply in its twisted rocks.

Daniel, a French teacher living in Namur and finishing his PhD, was a frequent visitor to the French department. Before handing in any of my written work, I asked him to look at it. He was intelligent and generous, but an alcoholic. Artistic in his writing, he always gave me a hard time. Whenever we disagreed, he exhibited a grammar book. He was looking for rules; I was looking for exceptions.

When he knew I was writing an essay on sexuality, he was adamant that he receive a copy. Each time we met, we went to a coffee bar where I often paid for his drink, Stella Artois.

'If Belgium can't be proud of anything,' he said, 'it still has the Artois. Don't invite me. Don't you know that I can't say "no"?'

When Daniel started to drink, he couldn't stop. Often, he became angry and aggressive if he were told he had crossed the line.

Daniel was a devout Catholic. A copy of the Bible was always in his valise. Reading my essay brought all his sexual misery to the fore.

'I like beer and dancing,' he told me. 'What I hate and can no longer bear is sex with no love.'

'This is not the same for everybody,' I told him. 'If one doesn't accept sex without love, few people would be married and very few children would be born.'

'I used to go dancing twice a week on Friday and Saturday. I managed to have sex with one or two, depending. I never felt great or good about it and went to confession every Sunday. My last time was the last. Leaving the dancehall, a girl and I went to a dark corner and had sex. I felt ashamed and guilty. I apologised to the girl. "Don't be daft!" she told me. "You are neither the first nor the last." That made me feel even worse.'

'That was just anticlimactic,' I told him.

'No. I did it with no love. It was like blind breeding, trying to impregnate a horse with a donkey. Why people call sex "love" when there is no love is beyond me.'

A middle-aged guru from India was invited to speak. 'Yoga and Brain: The Power of Breath' was the advertised title. Daniel refused to go to the talk. Maybe the time, 7 p.m., was wrong. The class was full of enthusiasts, students, academic staff and more. The room was warm, and the atmosphere seductive. Candles were in every corner and incense filled the room with clouds that had nowhere to go.

When the guru arrived, accompanied by the presenter, we all put our palms together and bowed our heads in the prayer position. He was substantial and broad-shouldered with well-exercised muscles. A thick, wide beard covered his cheeks and added to his girth. A long moustache shot out in both directions and a green ribbon criss-crossed his head. Pressed by his ribbon, his hair scattered all around his ears and covered his neck. He looked spiritual with a celestial power. The audience was mesmerised. For me, he was no more than a charlatan. Looking for love and happiness, the people of Louvain didn't know where to go. The further away it was, the more hope people had.

Not as everybody expected, the guru didn't utter a single word. Cross-legged, he sat on a red rug, facing us. He began inhaling and exhaling. We did as he did. We changed positions, extended our arms and stretched our legs. There wasn't always space. The touch of other people made some laugh, but others enjoyed it. The warmth of arms and legs of others made the room even more cosy. At the end, he suggested via the interpreter that we all lie on our tummies, a position unacceptable for me. It had a bad meaning in Morocco. It was a sexual and submissive position, acceptable only in the hospital and for medical reasons. I lay on my back. As it was the end of the day and left in this position for a while in the warm, stuffy room, I fell asleep. Apparently, I snored and made everybody giggle.

As the exercise finished, I left with a group of friends to have a coffee. We were seven: four boys and three girls. They had all come together, and it looked like they were dating. Connie was one of them.

'Did you sleep well?' Hans asked me. I saw his sarcastic smile.

'Did you enjoy the exercise?' I asked him.

'Fantastic!' he responded.

I shrugged, and Connie said, 'What did you dislike?'

'I couldn't lose myself in yoga, and certainly couldn't worship a man and hope for happiness in India,' I answered. 'A full happiness must have a door to the brain. The guru said nothing.'

'Door?' said Hans. 'Made with gold or steel?'

'Words are the door,' I told him.

Connie looked at me and gave me a broad smile. The others were all drinking beer, but Connie and I were drinking coffee. Hans liked arguing and winning.

'Why are words important?' he argued.

'On words, you can add, you can correct and correct the correction and so on. But you cannot paint over paint. If you do, it will be a different painting. You cannot write music over music. If you do, it will be chaos. But, with words, it's possible,' I said.

I got the impression Connie was delighted to hear me say that.

'The session of yoga was, for me, like getting into a shower, soaping myself, my hair, my entire body and then suddenly having no water to rinse. It was sticky,' I explained.

* . * *

HAVING A GRANT WAS JOYOUS, but it barely covered food and room. Dental fees were expensive, and a hygienist was unheard of. Extra jobs, an hour or two here and there, were life-support. A group of well-to-do students from the university and church decided to go skiing. They advertised for a cook to go to Zalamzi, Austria, for a week at Christmas and New Year. Interested, I replied.

'Two things one should never miss: a good friend and a Moroccan tagine,' I wrote. It was a small group of six men and six women, all in their late thirties and looking artificially matched. I travelled to Zalamzi on my own one night before them.

From Louvain to Munich was a full night's trip. From Munich to Zalamzi was a shorter distance, but the train was archaic. In Zalamzi, the accommodation was not a chalet, but a big centre populated with different groups, mainly Dutch and Americans. In a corner on the floor was a big bowl with a jug in the middle. I could not understand how it could be used. There was plenty of space outside, plenty of room, but not much space in the kitchen. Different groups, different messes. All people came there holding an umbrella: Christianity. I didn't.

My room was small with a single bed tucked against the wall. A glass window opened to the garden, covered with grass and dotted with trees. It gave the room a deceptive illusion of a wider space. With sun and snow, the glare was blinding. Arriving one night before them gave me a chance to explore the building and to find out where I was.

My group arrived at 1 p.m. on Christmas Eve. A misunderstanding erupted. They thought they had booked a five-star hotel, that Scottish bagpipes would be waiting to herald them in and a beautiful seductress would usher them to their rooms. They were shocked when they were handed their keys and ordered to find their rooms by following narrow, twisted corridors.

Jack blamed me for not trying to put the group all on one floor. I was furious. 'I didn't do the booking,' I said. 'Whoever did the booking should have requested all on one floor.'

'I did!' shouted Jack. 'I'm an engineer, not a hospitality expert. I didn't expect the cretins to spread us like seeds.'

As all eyes were glaring at him, he went on ranting and self-praising. *This is his culture*, I thought. *Be proud of what you have, exhibit your gifts; if you possess beauty, don't let it pass. I've heard that many times. It might have been transported from America. If you have nothing to say, at least shout.* That was what Jack did.

The storm passed, and we all went shopping before it got dark.

'I will cook one meal a day. The rest will be cold food: cheese, ham, bread, jam, salad, butter, eggs, mayonnaise and coffee, and for that everyone must pitch in,' I said.

We completely emptied the shelves, and the shopkeeper was happy and surprised.

Christmas Eve was exciting with good moods and good food. The gentlemen and the ladies threw on each other every charm they possessed. As the night went on, the boundary of properties disappeared. As the wine worked itself, the joy filled the room and bothered other neighbours. Bottle after bottle.

'It's Christmas Eve! It's Christmas Eve! Let's cheer and dance, cheer and dance. Let it be, let it be,' said Clare, singing and dancing. 'Love each other and love one another this Christmas Eve.'

Soon, everybody joined Clare. Six women turned into vampires, kissing everybody on their cheeks, chests and necks. They sucked every bit of blood from the men. The wine had messed up their minds and liberated their hearts. They all fell in love with the others' shadows. The shadow grew and there was no roof to restrain the love.

Christmas morning arrived on a galloping horse. The sleeping hours had been sweet, but very short. Because of the wine, there was no sign of life. Charged with breakfast, I was the first to get up. It was so quiet, I wondered if I were alone in the house. The kitchen was warm, but with a still air and malaise. It felt like an abattoir with large, wide sinks and big kitchen knives hanging on the wall.

Outside, the world was as it should be: Christmas Day. The ground was covered and subdued by the snow. The sky was wrapped in snow and dropping its best. The trees were white and all branches were tilting to the ground, so much snow had accumulated.

I turned on the urn, boiled the water and laid the table for twelve. Bread, cheese, butter and jam were on the table like an altar.

Looking for a warm, private place, Clare and Simone came to the kitchen to discuss the appalling conduct of Margaret, a petite, slim, brunette who had stolen the heart of Jack, Clare's partner.

'It was unmistakable that Jack was attracted to Margaret,' said Clare. 'She talked to him, kissed him, hugged him and big pig Jack enjoyed that. He ignored me and watched me watching them.'

Simone had nothing good to say about Barbara either. 'With her little voice, devil clothed like an angel, she sat on Luke's lap the entire night. She covered his face with her hair, didn't care if I was watching or not, and I don't know what else she could do,' said Simone.

Clare and Simone had come to the kitchen to decide what to do about the night that had turned out to be a disaster for them. All their conversation went to my ears, and I heard the two women angrily plotting.

It was almost midday and the rest of the group hadn't come for breakfast yet as expected. All three of us waited as we sat around the butcher table and drank coffee. Clare and Simone were both pharmacists, working in Brussels. Clare's father was a Belgian ambassador in Peru. Simone's parents were divorced, and her mother was a jewellery owner in Brussels, on a prestigious main street. Simone and Clare were not young chicks, but in their mid-thirties and let down by nature. As such, not many peacocks danced around them. If they did, they were lost quickly, as had happened last night.

Embittered, Clare lost the spirit of Christmas: love, forgiveness and giving. Her tongue turned into a burst tap of venom.

'I would kill Margaret if I could,' she said.

'You have already killed her,' I told her.

'How?' she asked.

'She has no loving existence in your heart any more. In your heart, she's dead. This is pretty sad,' I told her. 'Each one of us has a multitude of existences, life, death, in the same moment. It is this multitude which each of us needs. It either sustains our life or decreases our existence, not to mention the quality of life. Now, you are in Zalamzi, and half an hour ago, your father phoned you from Peru. You were in his mind. You were in his heart. Isn't that another "you" in him? In Peru? You are expecting a phone call from your mum in Brussels. Isn't that another existence of "you" in Brussels? You have killed Margaret. You are a loss for her.'

Either one by one or two by two, the group dripped in and filled the dining room, be it for late breakfast or early lunch. Everybody was subdued except Clare and Simone. They brought out two bottles of champagne and served everyone. There were no stockings or gifts, and if there had been, they'd been done privately.

Just as they had dripped in, they dripped out. I cleared the table, shouted for help, but everybody had something more important with which to be occupied than swimming in dishwater.

The snow didn't stop all afternoon, and I kept cooking until tea time. I had no contact with the group until the table was laid. I had cooked two big pots of meat and two big pots of rice.

To make the food I had promised, I had brought different spices with me: cumin, black pepper, sage, dill, rosemary and Italian seasoning. Using the same table and dining room, Simone and Clare decorated with glittering red candles and spread a dozen bottles of wine around.

Tagine and rice was the best Christmas meal for everybody that day, but accompanied with wine, it swelled the stomach and loosened faculties.

'Good chef! Good chef!' shouted everyone.

'But unhappy, unhappy,' I murmured to myself. I didn't belong. I felt alone. True, I had been hired as a cook, but this was Christmas Day, and I myself didn't believe in it. After such a copious dinner, the party really started, but that didn't help Clare and Simone. The time they spent serving wine and topping up glasses was a gift to their partners to enjoy kissing and hugging their new loves from the previous night. Again, Simone and Clare reaped a miserable evening. Their new make-up and their new clothes let them down for a second time.

I awakened in the morning and there was no sunrise or sunset to go by. The falling snow made Christmas Day and Boxing Day look like one and the same: identical twins. Looking outside from inside, I felt locked in, barred. For a while, I sat by the window and watched nature creating itself, writing its history, its drama and heralding its peril, just like a poet invaded with an emotion and not knowing what to do. Nature was dancing, one might say, but to whom? Everybody was in bed. I was awake, but the dance was not for me.

As though I were a piece of tile, designed to fill and fit a hole in the kitchen floor, my job was just breakfast. I filled two urns and laid the table. Bread, jam, butter, cheese, ham, coffee cups, napkins and all the necessary cutlery covered the entire table, yet it lacked charm. Neither Clare nor Simone showed up this morning. Midday passed, and no one descended. Frustrating.

Then, some arrived, dragging their feet in loose slippers, some in socks alone, and others with untied shoes.

'Unsmart feet are like bread with no butter,' I told Clare. 'It lacks taste.'

'It's how Boxing Day is,' she told me.

I packed my clothes and went to the main building. 'I am leaving,' I told Clare on the phone.

'What!?' she exclaimed.

'I am leaving.'

'You will be paid,' she said.

'I don't want it. I have a cultural malaise. I am lonely, and I don't fit in the group. I am sorry. Happy New Year, and I hope to see you maybe in Brussels.'

I ordered a local taxi and headed to the nearest station to go to Munich.

The road was just as torturous as the weather itself. At four o'clock, it was pitch-black. To get to the train station, the car wheels needed snow chains. The distance was short, but the time was long. In Munich, the train station was a camp of refugees.

'Cancelled! Cancelled!' filled the air. People, like ants, rushed from the platform just to be told they were in the wrong place. Not every traveller spoke German. Unable to cope with the weather conditions, travellers kept asking questions. Families dragged their children as if the shadow of death were catching them. Most of them were from the communist bloc.

Ten o'clock in the morning, yet no train to Brussels. Whatever was advertised or programmed was false.

'Germans were more skilled and organised in killing innocent people than facing the snow and defeating the weather!' shouted an angry traveller.

At two thirty, my train moved, but inside were no seats. Pushing and shoving was the game of the night. I was, however, happy just to leave Armageddon behind.

18

From a few days before Christmas until a few days after New Year's, Leuven Street's shops, restaurants and bars all played classical music. Modern music wasn't on the menu. Instead, Handel, Mozart and Beethoven all competed to seduce and pull in the shoppers. While my feet were on the ground, wet and full of mud, my brain stretched itself like an eagle's wings and preyed on the music. This was the world I had left and exchanged for money. It had been like riding a horse with no saddle. It had been fun to begin with, but became awkward and ended sour. I had gone to Zalamzi in the hope of coming back with some money.

My sister Rabbia was now free and constantly wrote to me, breaking my heart and asking for money. My being in Europe made her, and many others where she lived, believe that Europe was abundant, just like many Europeans thought America was a pot of gold. Juggling education with a job had been my fate all along. A third of my grant went to her, but the hope was no hope. Constantly hunting for a job in a foreign land where I felt despised was not a blessing.

On the twenty-eighth of December, I found a job in a Chinese restaurant. I was delighted. Speaking Tarifit was difficult; it wore and tore the tongue and throat, but listening to Chinese people mesmerised me. The sound came from the back and the top of the throat.

The restaurant was not terribly hygienic, but the food was tasty. They had the magic. They never overcooked their vegetables, and mushrooms were an essential ingredient, the chef told me.

In charge of the dining room, I was asked to make a table for seven from ten until twelve in the evening. The restaurant was packed and the kitchen flooded with workers.

Surprise! At 10 p.m. promptly, Connie arrived with four men and two other women. I had the pleasure to seat and serve them. They were a hard group; unfamiliar with Chinese food, they bombarded me with questions. I was no more knowledgeable than they were. I kept shuttling back and forth between them and the kitchen.

The chef shouted at me as if I should know what was on the menu. I went back and advised them to order and share. Thankfully, they bought the idea. A Chinese lady, an expert in wine, populated the table with some exclusive, expensive bottles.

Not long after ordering, the mixed group began to flirt with each other, all except Connie. She didn't take any part in the wine drinking, and I wondered why. She was a nun, a student, far from her order, and she had all the freedom to do and go. Keeping my eyes on the table, I talked to her, maybe too much.

The owner came and whispered into my ear, 'Too much talk. We're busy.'

I kept talking to her and as the time went on, she looked

disconnected from the group. Unhappy with me, the owner took me to the kitchen.

Demotion. The kitchen was small and hot. Workers were like surgeons in the operating theatre. Being in the kitchen, I was cut off from Connie and her group. At 1 a.m., the restaurant was still packed.

'Someone wants to talk to you!' the owner shouted at me.

Moving to reception and with a huge white chef's hat on my head, almost a sign of disgrace, I found Connie waiting for me. Smiles emanated from both sides.

'Would you like us to have a dinner tomorrow?' she asked.

'Yes. Where?' I asked.

'Do you like curry?'

'Yes.'

'Then the Indian restaurant,' she said.

No kisses, but a loose hug, and she rejoined the group.

We worked until four in the morning. Had the restaurant more seating space, it would have tripled its revenue.

At 8 p.m. on the twenty-ninth of December, I went to the top of the hill where the Indian restaurant served academic students and public alike. Neither of us had to come from far away. I arrived first, stood in the street and waited for Connie.

She arrived looking very smart, wearing black boots, a long black skirt and a red pullover with a red scarf. We sat at a table and faced each other for the first time. She was far more relaxed than I was. Sometimes my mind let me down. I thought of my PhD, my financial difficulties, my sister. Too many wounds and too many scars. Poor concentration. Luckily, this didn't affect her.

When she wanted to know more about me, I told her, 'My name is Mohammed. I am the great-great-great-great-great-grandson of Mohammed, the Prophet, peace be upon Him.'

She found that funny, unbelievable and ridiculous. I had a certificate in my pocket, yanked it out and handed it to her. She patiently read the entire document and looked at me, her eyes frozen.

'Are you special?' she asked.

'No.'

'Then what?' she questioned.

'That is just who I am, the great-great-great-great-great-grandson of Mohammed, the Prophet, peace be upon Him.'

'If you were to ask me who I am, I would say, "From Fresno. I was born there, lived there, went to primary and secondary school there, then I moved to Berkeley. I worked in the bank, and I hated it. Then, I joined the sister order. We are a small group; some of us teach and some work as nurses. We are all supposed to do something, be active and a member of the bigger community. We are allowed to care, but not love."'

'Why?' I asked.

'We are only allowed to love Jesus,' she explained.

'Lucky boy,' I told her.

To change the subject, I said, 'Jacques Lacan is giving a conference tomorrow.'

'Who is he?' she asked.

'He's a French psychiatrist, well known. He's not easy to understand, but many other psychiatrists are going to the conference. Scott, the Belgian psychiatric guru, will certainly be there.'

'Are you not working tomorrow?' she asked.

'No. The conference is related to my subject. It starts at 7 p.m.'

'That sounds very interesting. I might go as well,' she said. When it came time to pay the bill, she refused my offer. I insisted.

'No! Dutch treat,' she said adamantly.

We left the restaurant with a mutual hug, warm and disturbing.

I went to my room, haunted. Something. Just something. Sweet. Invisible and nonpalpable, like perfume. So strong, but just in the air. *Where did it come from, and where is it going?*

As expected, the theatre was packed with people of arts and science. Some were lucky to find a seat, while others stood, forming a half-moon.

Lacan arrived walking slowly and with extreme confidence. He had a bow tie on his white shirt. The moment he opened his mouth, a man jumped onto the stage, grabbed the microphone and pushed him away. Lacan stayed poised and calm, obviously used to mentally disturbed people. Restrained, the attacker was shoved out into the street.

I listened to Lacan with all my energy, trying to get as much as I could. There was a bit for everybody, but not enough for anyone. At the end, I grabbed the opportunity and put my view to him.

'Consciousness is not a creek, even when eyes are open and the ears stretched,' I said.

'This is a negative definition. What is the positive?' he asked.

'Consciousness is an infinite, a small bulb of light distributed in an infinite, dark space,' I answered. 'The bulbs steal light from each other, and the darkness gets thick with the understanding that the darkness is dynamic, full of contradictory waves.'

As the talk ended, the wine travelled far and fast. One hand holding a glass, the other a pipe or a cigarette, everybody engaged in either smiling or laughing, which made any useful conversation difficult to hear and, if one did, hard to understand.

In this cheery and crowded atmosphere, I tried to find Connie. Disappointed, I thought my hope was out of place.

I had never celebrated New Year's or even knew what people did. I assumed, however, that food, drink and sex were the essence of it.

This year was an exception. Getting out on the thirty-first of December, I found an invitation to celebrate the New Year. Who was the host? Not knowing didn't stop me from going.

A devout Catholic couple, the husband, a lecturer, and the wife, a psychologist, had decided to open their home for foreigners like me, who otherwise would be stuck in their rooms or, at best, in a pub. I was the first arrival. Other guests began to drip in, each with a present, a bottle of wine, chocolates, cake, and some with flowers. Empty-handed, I felt extremely embarrassed, and going out to bring something would make me look totally odd. Connie arrived with her friends. I expected she had initiated the invitation.

The evening was smooth. I spoke to the host. He had just come from teaching engineering in the United States.

'Do you like the United States?' I asked.

'No,' he answered. 'You hardly ever meet anyone intelligent outside the university.'

'Do they do much better teaching than here?'

'No.'

'What about research?' I asked.

'They are not much better than us, but they have an enormous budget; a lot of money goes down the drain. If here, a project involves one or two researchers, in the United States, you would have one hundred. What about Morocco?' he asked.

'We're in a deep coma.'

Overhearing me, Connie butted in. 'But you are not.'

I couldn't help but smile at her. The food was abundantly spread all around on different tables for everyone to eat what he liked, drink what he wanted and sit wherever he desired. Connie and I sat on a small sofa, physically close. When I wanted her attention, I tapped on her shoulder, never on her thigh. Occasionally, she tapped on my leg. She was far more cultured than I was. She evoked art, music, architecture, and I knew nothing. To counter my ignorance, I spoke of my work. She sounded interested and was a good listener.

'I don't know how to type,' I told her.

'If you have anything to type, I will do that for you,' she offered.

'My handwriting isn't good,' I added.

'I will cope.'

Now and again, we moved around and were soon back to the sofa. She had a glass of wine when she arrived. It stayed in her hand until midnight.

Twenty of us from all different corners of the world stood in a circle and waited for the new year at twelve midnight. The arithmetic was easy. Twenty people, nineteen kisses, except when it was male to male. It was an occasion. Idiots would miss it.

I kissed no one except Connie, and twice, once on each cheek. She did the same. When I left, I went farther. I kissed her on her lips. This was the only time in my entire life that my lips had been in contact with a girl's lips. It was memorable, but it was devoid of any erotic nature. I have kept this kiss in my memory to this day in my life. It was not one thousand and one nights, but one night of one thousand and one nights.

I never expected or wanted to get close to a woman after Khadija. Suspicious of them, they frightened me. Did I need a psychiatrist? Or should I just do what everybody else did, push and see what I could get from this beautiful lady, Connie? The reality was she was very good, and I was a believer, with a strong faith. I liked her.

*   *   *

LATER IN THE YEAR, I went to Utrecht. Professor Kuant agreed to see me. Utrecht was not too far from Belgium, but the weather was atrocious, still winter. He saw me not at the university, but at his own house. It was a terraced home facing a wide road. His wife served us coffee all the time I was there. She looked much younger than he. Apparently, she was still his student. He had been a priest and had abandoned everything.

I had gone to see Professor Kuant and had learned that we spoke different languages, though we spoke of the same topic.

He had read Merleau-Ponty's original text in French, then had put his understanding into English. My chore was to understand them both and add my contribution to it, in French.

Coming back, I was hit by a severe migraine. I had to interrupt my journey and spend the night in the nearest possible hotel. I went straight to bed. If I had learned anything from Kuant, it was that languages, even when they try to say the same things, end up being like a horse caught in a race. If a naked girl were put on a bed under equal light from every direction, and one were to commission two painters to submit their drawings, one would see different legs, different arms, different cheeks, different colours, different breasts, let alone the impression, because it would be subjective like language, love and sex. Two languages could never say the same things.

19

Easter came and brought with it many changes: more sunny days, the grass growing, trees leafing, and even the worms under the ground starting to move. It was also a spiritual time. Christians glorified Easter. They trapped their faith tightly, like in a capsule, in resurrection. The resurrection story was the big bang for them. Whatever happened to the goose would happen to the gander. Jesus had either resurrected Himself or had been resurrected. Whoever believed in Him would have the same fate.

One needed a large bucket of faith. That I didn't have. I didn't need. At Easter, Taize, France, Rome, and Jerusalem were the destinations for many I knew in Louvain. Spirituality, holiday, adventures were a mixed bag.

Connie didn't go anywhere, but invited me to Brussels. First, to go to a church service, then to have a dinner with a well-to-do German woman. Her name was Elizaloth. There wasn't a better place to get to know Connie than on the train. From Louvain, we took the train on Thursday morning.

In Brussels, I had never been out of the station. All I knew was that it was a big city. I was blind, and Connie was the torch. The journey was short, but to get there, we had to cross some dark, dismal streets. When Connie invited me, I had expected some majestic cathedral, to see a procession of priests in white and red and to hear an organ, a sound that would lift my brain to heaven. This place was not a cathedral, house or garage. It was a large hall with no Jesus statues, no Mary statues or any pictures. Jews, Christians and Muslims all had a sanctuary. This hall didn't have one. I had read and seen pictures of the Vatican, its paintings, wealth and beauty. This place, this hall, was not part of it. Its capital was chairs, four walls and doors.

Connie sat down first. Beside her, I sat watching her. She yanked a small black Bible from her black bag, slowly leafed through and read a few words. Then, she closed her eyes, her right palm on her left hand, tilted her head down to the floor and dove into silent, personal prayer. Beside her, I sat and gazed around, watching people quietly coming in. They all emulated Connie.

This is far more serious that I thought, I mused. *Am I in another* zawiya? More than twenty minutes passed, and Connie was still in the same position. No movement but steady breathing. I became anxious and prepared myself to leave. *Yes, no, go, stay*, became loud music in my mind. For the first time, Connie lifted up her right hand and put it on my left thigh. Now, I felt shackled.

A man came, and with a few words, he revived everybody — except me. All necks and heads moved backwards. Coming back from her secret world, Connie kept her hand on me, but I was as cold as a fish.

The speaker, a lay man respectfully clothed, but not in Prada or Gucci, began to speak with a mellifluous, strong voice. No theology, no philosophy or settled creed. No heaven or hell. Yet, he said something. Not inspired from novels, movies, but from a small book he called *The New Testament*. It was a relief for me to get free from this ordeal.

As we left, we took the tram to Elizaloth's. Before reaching her flat, not wanting to be too early, we stopped for a coffee.

Connie, sensitively intelligent, felt I was lost in space and mind. With coffee on the table, we faced each other and she asked, 'Did you enjoy the morning?'

'No,' I replied, coldly.

'I understand,' she said. 'I'm going to explain something. I hope you will understand. I am not a nun, but a Christian. Before leaving the United States, I thought I should wear a ring. Then I settled on this idea to just say I am a nun. Being my age, a mature student, I didn't want to be harassed. I didn't want to be invited, but I want to be free. From the day I told you I am a nun, when we had just met and you made those controversial remarks, I have felt uncomfortable with you each time we've met. I could have worn a ring, but then you might have shied away from me.' She paused.

No matter how much I had learned, books I had read or contacts I had made, my culture, mixed with my religion, Islam, was my id, ego and superego. Connie was sincere and looked stunningly beautiful. She had found a solution, a wall, to protect her dignity and pride; me, I needed to destroy a thicker wall than hers to reach where she was firmly residing. Looking at me, she reached her hand, palm up, and with no words, she invited me to join her. I put my hand into her palm. I paid for the coffee, and she bought a packet of Belgian chocolates for Elizaloth.

Elizaloth's flat was modern and on an affluent street. When we arrived, she looked surprised to see me. She gazed at me, looked at Connie and said, 'Is this man with you? Your friend?'

'Yes,' Connie replied, looking slightly embarrassed. 'He came with me. We both went to the church.'

A smile broke onto Elizaloth's cheeks, but all the time that I was there, I was subject to an invasive gaze. Two guests had already arrived before us. They were both British. The woman was from Wales and the man was from England.

Elizaloth was conscious and proud of her flat. Because of what she had achieved, coming from Germany destitute, she wanted every guest to know that. She constantly referred to her past and where she was now. She was a fussy woman; she didn't like to be crowded when cooking, nor did she accept help. Things had to be her own way, including dishwashing.

Elizaloth was extremely generous. The huge turkey overflowed its platter on the table, and there were many different vegetables and gravy. An assortment of cakes was served with fresh double cream, accompanied with carafes of filtered coffee.

Most of the time, the conversation was in English. I was the odd one out. I tried my best to follow the flow, but caught only every fifth word, if that. During the conversation, Elizaloth in particular, never referred to herself as 'I'.

'God sent me such and such person to meet me in the shop. God delayed the train for me to go to Frankfurt. God told me to get rid of this mattress,' she said.

Elizaloth is a new chapter in psychiatry, I thought. *This is worse than fatalism. Some people want to be too religious and end by being anti-religious. As all comes from God, Elizaloth can never be wrong. She is sinful. I thought the idea of God had only some meaning if there were a little freedom. Without it, the idea of God is senseless. Only because of this little freedom can man have some relationship with God, and only because of this little freedom, God cannot escape what man thinks of Him.*

Elizaloth was not stupid. She was in her late fifties and had a French lover, married and older than she, but 'he is not a flesh lover,' she said. Hearing her talking about him, I found it difficult to think of a Frenchman as 'not a flesh lover'.

By the end of the afternoon, I felt tired, not used to the rich and excessive food that I had consumed. Connie and I left Elizaloth and took the last train to Louvain. On our way, we sat side by side, emotionally on the brink of understanding each other.

Connie never rejected my hand whenever I reached for hers. Financially, I was on life support, though beneficiary of a small grant.

Connie was living with nuns, though she was not one. While nuns were helping, they were also securing an income. I left her at the convent. The university edict didn't allow male students to visit females and vice versa.

Taking care of my studies, constantly looking for part-time jobs to make ends meet and having some time with Connie became stressfully difficult. Connie was now out of the closet. People saw us hand in hand in a restaurant or café. Losing her to another was my worst fear. On the material side, I had nothing to offer. On a spiritual level, she was a devout Christian and, equally, I was a devout Muslim.

20

The years 1973 and 1974 were a torturous time for me. As I worked – still – on my PhD, my grant abruptly came to its end. The Yom Kippur War shaped the entire world's economy. Some governments ran out of money and froze any recruitment. Some universities did the same. Inflation soared, some countries almost ran out of energy, and even the almighty United States rationed petrol. People ran out of fuel, and some died trying to siphon petrol from others' tanks.

My grant was cut, and I found it very difficult to find any job. I changed accommodation and moved to a very, very small room, three by two metres, bare and with no heating, electric or gas. By this time, my relationship with Connie was intense and emotionally deep. She liked conferences and talks, especially religious or political, and she didn't want to go alone. Neither did I.

A German speaker, an academic from the University of Heidelberg, was invited to talk. Like many, we went to hear him. He spoke about saints and defined holiness in passive terms: not doing the wrong things. I put my hand up and objected.

'Holiness,' I said, 'should be defined in positive terms, or what is done.'

What I said excited Connie. Her objection was like spitting fire. 'There are no saints,' she said, 'just sinners. As long as we are sinners, we can't be holy. No one will ever be.'

All the time she was arguing, she felt hot and sweaty, holding my hand very tightly in hers. Whatever was the value of the arguments, I saw once again how she was rooted in her faith. She had a block of ideas as solid as a stone and intertwined. No one could knock her stone down or even chip it.

Not well-connected with her feelings at that time, I said, 'I might do the aggregation after my PhD.'

'Then, when are you going to finish?' she asked.

'Whenever you want it,' I replied.

'You are not Christian yet. You know that I love you, but I can't be a Muslim wife.' *Can't be a Muslim wife.* This sentence threw me into the past and the future. Since I'd met Connie, the time had felt for her and me like a cotton ball: soft, cuddly and with nothing on it to hurt. It had felt like a sweet in my mouth; it didn't melt. The tongue played with it, left and right, but it remained sweet, never bitter.

We sat side by side, hand in hand, but the shadow of the future was terrifying. On our backs, two vampires, her religion and mine, were sucking the blood out of us.

Connie's time in Louvain came to its end; she had finished her studies; her loan and grant had run out. She bought a ticket from Brussels to Chicago. At the airport, we both looked at the moon and hoped for the dawn, that one vampire might turn into a tick, get full and fall off.

Devoured, I couldn't cope. My heart was shattered into pieces. The counsellor was my tears, flood after flood.

Suddenly, the sun eclipsed and the moon hid. I found myself like a painter with one single colour: black. Painting black over black created no light or contrast.

Watching Connie leaving and my staying behind isn't the right thing, I thought. *We should either both fly or both stay.*

Not being Christian had not been my choice or my decision. If it had been so, my faith would have been a bargaining process, a currency to trade. I had not been called into the Christian faith.

21

Work, work, work was my consolation. Yet, the time stretched into infinity. Hours became days, and days became weeks. With a divided heart and divided mind, that was how I lived. It was hard to resew them. Connie had left me with a Bible, and I had promised to read it.

Two weeks passed and there was no news from her yet. I wrote to her every day. *Is she okay?* I wondered. *Was someone else waiting for her?*

On fire, I went to see Professor Dewealheus. I nervously handed him my manuscript. I had no idea what he was going to tell me or suggest. He was very difficult, demanding and impossible to predict. Reading manuscripts took time. Months.

A few days later, walking in the street, I met a student friend. Before saying anything, he told me that the professor wanted to see me.

In a hurry, I made an appointment via telephone and went to see him at his home. It was lunchtime, and his wife was cooking cheese. An enormous aroma was escaping from the house, and I was hungry.

'I started to read your manuscript, thinking I would come back to it later when I came back from Paris. But, interested,

I took it with me and read it on the train,' he told me. He was quite curious. 'How did you get to that conclusion? Where did you find it? You should be happy and proud of your work.'

I went immediately to register for submission of my thesis.

* * *

BEING TOLD YOU WERE A 'foreigner' was never a pleasant sound. The word was not benign. I always wondered what and how much people packed into the word 'woman'. Was it simply anatomy? Certainly not. It was social, religious, emotional, etc. The word 'foreigner', '*étranger*', 'outlander' and 'woman' had a lot in common.

In the region from where I had come, we called women '*thamgarth*', signifying inferiority. Politely, 'inequality'. One had to be ready to duke it out if one called a male person '*thamgarth*'. To prove he was not, he wouldn't exhibit his penis, but would turn himself into a vicious bull terrier.

'Foreigner', 'étranger', 'outlander' intrinsically carried inequality. It was not a matter of law, black and white, but a matter of perception. It was not a matter of competence. Competence could be tested, but not perception. Perception overrode the law. It always found its way. Religion had been obsessed about the relationship between man and God, and rightly so, but not by the equality between man and woman. One day maybe that would happen. If it did, I would change the word '*thamgarth*' to '*ariẓe*' ('man'). Man and woman would be one single colour, but deeply, deeply red like oxblood.

*　*　*

AFTER EIGHT YEARS OF INTENSE study at Louvain University and armed with a Master of Arts, PhD and Aggregation, I was offered jobs in Bengazi and Rabat. I chose the latter, though for significantly less money. I joined the Faculty of Arts, University of Rabat, as *maitre du conference*. The faculty was in turmoil and filled with leftists. The dean had the power of life and death, recruiting and sacking. In my time in the Faculty of Arts, you would not know if you were in Rabat or in Cairo. Egyptian professors and their Egyptian dialect filled the rooms and corridors. This was a reaction to a time when French had filled the faculty. One group was out and another in.

The dean, Jaffar Kittani, filled the faculty with Egyptians, and many Moroccans were sent home on payroll. After several months, I was told the Louvain diplomas were not recognised, not accepted. Then I was made a civilian, the opposite of a military job. This new status gave me no benefit of wage whatsoever from my diplomas. Some degrees were accepted, depending on who you were.

I was always hoping for the best. When the new dean, Mohammad Kabli, took over, he brought a clique of socialists who had been sent home by the previous dean. They terrorised whoever didn't share their views. Mr Kabli had never written anything. Purely an academic tube.

'How many pages did your PhD have?' he asked me. 'How long did it take?'

'It isn't a matter of pages or weight,' I told him. 'I offered it to you to read. It's already in the library.'

22

In 1975 and 1976, the Faculty of Arts in Rabat was a sinkhole. Infighting, gossip, clique warfare and self-flattering filled the life of the building. Cronyism was at its peak. 'My diploma is much better than his,' was heard. No research or publications were there to support the claims. If it were possible, socially acceptable, one would hear, 'My ass is much better than his.' Deep down, I found the atmosphere disappointing, shocking and academically choking.

Waiting month after month to receive my civilian wage, my finances reached an alarming point. Renting a studio was beyond my ability. I rented a room in a dilapidated building owned by an Italian landlord. The room had no water, and the common toilet was constantly blocked. To have a shower, I had to walk a few miles to the public baths. My academic work in Louvain had led me to a catastrophe.

I wrote to the University of Louvain, and the chancellor was furious. Louvain degrees were sought and respected worldwide, and particularly in philosophy. He wrote via the diplomatic channels, even threatening to take the issue to the United Nations. It was not a matter of one person's PhD. It was a matter of the entire university. The people who supervised the job were the academic giants of Europe. They were deeply insulted. Hundreds of professors all over the world who had the same qualification were concerned. However, it made no difference to Mohammad Kabli.

He acted as minister and turned the faculty into a sub-political party. If advice were needed, he resorted exclusively to his political clique, a mix of left and hard left. I had no political inclination. I was not only marginalised; I was rejected. But I refused to give up. Other professors invited me to stand in for them.

Professor Kamila, an Egyptian from the University of Cairo, asked me to stand in for him. In his place, I delivered several lectures to different classes and students, who went straight to the dean and demanded that I lecture again. That, too, made no difference.

After several weeks in a row, I began to know students, their names, their grades and sometimes their ambitions. Some were always late. They were either teachers nearby or in other jobs.

A student with tinted glasses, always sitting in the same place near the window, scarf around her neck, looking middle-aged unlike the rest of the class, was always the first; she sometimes took notes and sometimes just gazed at the blackboard. I had to rush immediately after class to the School of Safety and Hygiene where I offered a few lectures, as I had no transport.

Coming out of the building, I had several books stacked under my arm. The front faculty car park was choked with cars, most of them facing the building. Serpentining was the only way to pass. Not far away there was a row of parked vehicles, people squirming to get out. The student in my class who constantly wore tinted glasses and was sometimes writing, sometimes dreaming, came toward me. She was wearing black trousers, a casual jacket, scarf around her neck and the tinted glasses covering her entire eyebrows. I dodged her. In a way I couldn't pass, she faced me. Not knowing what to do or say, I stayed put. Suddenly, she tore off her glasses.

'Are you Jusef?' she asked.

'Yes,' I answered, in a perplexed voice.

'Do you not recognise me?' she asked.

'No.'

The smile that she had had on her face disappeared and her colour changed. Fright. 'I am Khadija,' she said. 'You were my sweetheart. Do you remember baccalaureate time?'

As if no time had passed, the past became the present. *This is Khadija, my high school sweetheart.* She put her arms around me, and I returned her hug. We both cried. We hadn't seen each other for many years and had gone different ways.

She was crying so much, I couldn't stop her. All her make-up melted down and trickled down her face. She looked a bit older, but still beautiful.

She looked at me and suggested we meet for a coffee in the town. It was, for me, a disturbing time. I didn't want to step back into the past. The present was bitter enough. Going back would mean a rebirth of struggle, yet I agreed to meet her in Palima, a chic hotel in the new town and built in the time of French colonialism. It had an open terrace facing the main avenue.

During this time, I was deciding on two roads: either to emigrate to the United States or go to England to further my study by doing a second PhD. It wasn't Oxford or Cambridge I should choose, but where a minister or his relatives had gone. Those people wrote the law. Their shadow was power enough to split the ocean. Following their path and going where they had gone would be the wisdom of the wise.

While waiting to meet Khadija, my mind bubbled and worried. She was a married woman. There was no asexual relationship between a man and a woman in Morocco. At least, this was how we grew up to think and behave. It was not always men. Moroccan women could be hot, veiled or unveiled. Before meeting Khadija, I had already complexed myself, though it was with great pleasure I wanted to see her.

On the hotel terrace, I anxiously waited for her. I peered through strolling pedestrians. When I spied her, I left my chair and met her at the bottom stair. Smiles, shining teeth, pupils and hair as dark as ever. We met with colliding hugs. I consciously dodged her face. If she had expected a kiss, it didn't happen. I wasn't fit for it. We went back to my table, not hand in hand as lovers, but as friends with a distance between us.

I had already ordered tea. 'I am always craving strong coffee,' she said. We sat not side by side, but across from each other. She drank coffee, cuddled the cup, secured between her palms as though it might fly. Her fingers, wrists, neck and ears were all jewellery-free. This was not the tradition of her mother or mine. Being jewellery-free was an open page into history, several years in school where everything was sweet. Dreams and hopes coated the future and crushed all obstacles.

'We were in the same class and shared the same dreams. You ended up at the university, and I as a primary school teacher,' she said.

'You are married. I am still single and alone,' I said.

'I am a divorcee, married with no purpose or love.'

I really didn't want to dig into Khadija's private life. She had broken my dream. Maybe this had been just a teenager's dream.

'Where do you teach?' I asked her.

'*Y, Monsour*,' she responded

'From Fes to Rabat, what has brought you here?' I asked.

'Complex story,' she said. 'As a divorcee, I have to support myself and two boys. The younger one has Down's syndrome.'

'Is it family related?' I asked.

'Yes,' she said.

'Maybe cousins shouldn't be allowed to marry,' I told her.

Pause. Sorrow behind the smile.

'That would tear the fabric of the family,' she said.

'From the North where I came, children are married before they are born. It's like reserving a seat or putting jewellery in the vault. What is your ex-husband doing?' I asked.

'Still in the bank,' she responded.

'Did you marry your cousin with love?' I asked. I realised this was a difficult question. I was afraid of the answer in case she said 'yes'. If so, all the sweet time at school was just an escape. For me, it wasn't. The sorrow behind her smile was constant.

'Would you like to come for tea to see my children?' she asked.

'You live with your mother. She used to chase me,' I replied.

'She wouldn't do that this time,' she said.

I had no intention of seeing her mother. She used to give me bad looks, despise me, slam the door on me, tell me lies, and she had kept Khadija for her brother's son.

'When did you get divorced?' I asked.

'Six years ago. I did one year's training and became a primary teacher after that,' she answered. 'I left Fes and with it, the tribe. In the tribe, you never know who you are.'

We spent three hours talking, me mostly listening to her. I needed to go, as I had two jobs. She didn't seem to be in a hurry. We parted. Leaving, I saw her wiping her tears. My heart nearly stopped.

23

Teaching at the art faculty, Rabat, in 1975–1976 was like riding in a rodeo. One second you were up, and the next second, you were on the ground. The lack of structure meant chaos. Departments had no head and, worse, no professors with precise specialties. The faculty had no council, nor did the university. The dean, appointed by His Majesty the King, held all the power. The rest, only to sing doo-wops.

At that time, the dean's position was held by Jaffar Kittani and Mohammad Kabli. Neither of them had left any academic track, inside the library or outside the library. Cronyism and incompetence were their fortes. I wasn't happy to do so little and spend my time in the sun and strolling in the street.

I was leaving the library and going down to the town when Khadija caught up with me, as if we had come out of the college and no time had passed. We went to a café across from the train station. It was once — and still was — a spot for lovers. French had come here, wined, dined and kissed. It was a curious spot for Moroccans. They came, peered through the window and wondered what was next.

'My time as a civilian is coming to its end. I am leaving, either to the United States or United Kingdom,' I told Khadija.

'That can't be true,' she said.

'It's not a matter of the degree, university, qualification or competence. It's a club mentality. Corrupt. It's financially cliquey,' I said.

'Can you not join the club?' she asked.

'You might join the club, but before long, they will shake you up and down, empty you of any personal worth. They will reduce you to a parrot. You say "black" when in the front of you is white, and you say "white" when in the front of you is dark,' I said.

'Try to piss from the inside out. It's much better than pissing from the outside in,' she responded.

'I will keep pissing until either my bladder gets empty or they get wet,' I said.

A friend of mine with a diplomatic background in Madrid advised me not to go to any university, but to Southampton. 'A social giant,' he said, 'graduated from that university. No dean would take a risk and mess with that giant.'

He was right.

To go to England or the United States, I needed English. Coming from the north of Morocco, I had already struggled to learn the Moroccan dialect, Arabic language and French. Now, English.

A Swedish midwife helped me to fill the application for both Southampton and Berkeley. Her typewriter was archaic, the letters almost invisible, and her English was pretty bad. I applied to do research. Both universities offered me a place. I chose the United Kingdom. Whatever I had, books, clothes or furniture had to go, not that I had very much. I started a journey with no horizon.

During this tumultuous time, I hid myself in reading, with a particular curiosity of the Bible. I found it full of stories, ups and downs. Full of twists. It hit me like God and man teasing each other.

I was not interested in theology, man's construction, but God and man dancing a tango. Man got tired and withered, then went, but not God. I wondered how long He would play? Soon He would be alone. I had no theology to go by, just faith. The film *Jesus Christ Superstar* struck me as a book that said everything, yet with nothing specific to refute. Jesus, a man, just like us, lost and wading, but was something more. On that, I built my faith: a new faith.

24

Man's problems weren't always political or religious. Often, they were personal, individual. No political system or religion could provide a complete fence against the bullies, corrupt and immoral. They were everywhere. It was all in the heart. Though I had a huge problem to distinguish between action and intention, I cherished Jesus's idea. The desire, idea, thought or intentionality was as powerful as the action itself. Evil was not a concept, idea, a mathematical number, but an energy. No capsule was strong and powerful enough to contain it. Worse, it was like a cancer cell. It didn't work alone. It recruited from healthy cells to ravage. Evil could only be challenged by action. Studying more, for me, was the only weapon to penetrate the castle.

Learning English was difficult. It required money and time. The British Consul and the American School charged a lot. The chemistry of English didn't allow self-teaching. One might do, but end up not speaking English. It required human voice, human correction.

I struggled, made a dent and borrowed money from my sister living in Holland, but I didn't have the money to pay the university fee, though accepted, thanks to Professor Manser.

I managed to rent a room from a Rabat rabbi. He was an estate agent and well known. Moroccan landlords trusted him, and he paid them back. Kindly, he allowed me to forward my correspondence to his address, as I had never had a permanent residence or knew when I would leave. I had a nomadic life in the heart of the capital. Trusting no one, the rabbi collected the rent himself on behalf of the landlord. He never came in the early morning or in the afternoon, but always during lunch time, to make sure the tenants would be there.

He once came to collect the rent and brought some junk correspondence, but with it, a letter from Connie. I hadn't received a word from her for a while. Being coiled, retreated, in my problems, I just wrote to her sporadically and maybe with a cold pen, expecting nothing. She was in the United States; I was in Morocco and on my way to England. The envelope was thick. I wondered what was in it. The rabbi left, smiling, rent in hand, and in a hurry, I tore open the envelope to read the letter.

The letter was several pages and had a real dried flower crushed inside. The spring flower of America was in my hand. Reading her letter, my mind fizzed off. She wrote:

I will be in Rabat in three weeks. I want to see you, talk to you and, if you allow it, hug you!!! I will stay with some Americans; some are missionaries, others not. They will pick me up from Casablanca airport. My itinerary will be New York, London then Casablanca.

Is this just to see me? To do something? Tourist? I wondered. To come to Rabat was entirely her own decision.

American people might be modest and ordinary in the United States, but not in Rabat. Connie gave me the address of Mr and Mrs McGraw. I searched to find their home. Before reaching their house, I recognised where they lived: big house, American cars and a fierce dog trying to jump out. I was worried that I might be suspicious, a currency in the capital. I rang the bell and held Connie's letter in my hand, making me look like a postman.

A female maid came straightaway and shouted from behind the gate, 'What?'

'I want to speak to Mr and Mrs McGraw,' I answered.

'Tell me what you want to tell them,' she demanded.

'I have a letter,' I said.

'Give it to me. I will pass it to them.'

'No, I can't,' I responded.

After a barrage, she called Mrs McGraw. They both rushed to the gate. Mrs McGraw was first. She was short, heavily built, strong and broad-shouldered, with fair skin, a ruddy complexion, short blonde hair and rimless glasses. Her husband was tall, dwarfing her, thin, with heavy glasses and a generous moustache.

'I am a friend of Connie,' I told them. 'Here is her letter. She is going to come to stay with you. I want to present myself and make sure that I know where she is and that's she's safe.'

Mrs McGraw was very polite. She invited me in while her husband tried to control their black bull terrier. She took me to a huge lounge, richly decorated, looking out onto the grove with oranges, lemons, limes and grapefruit. A lot of noise was coming in as two male gardeners were mowing. Mrs McGraw showered me with questions while the maid was percolating coffee. Before questioning, she told me that she was from Colorado and had lived in Kenya. She sounded very familiar with African culture, and more than I was.

'How did you get to know Connie?' she asked.

'I met her during a debate in Louvain.'

'Debate?' she asked.

'Many,' I answered. 'She seemed to be interested and fascinated.' As I didn't have more to tell, we moved on to usual topics, like religion, politics, economy. Talk for talk's sake.

Mr and Mrs McGraw were supposed to meet Connie at the Casablanca airport. I convinced them that they didn't need to.

'How will you get there?' asked Mrs McGraw.

'From Rabat, I will take the train. Coming back, I will hire a taxi.'

'Expensive,' she said.

'Not compared to Connie's expense,' I answered.

Connie landed at the Casablanca airport in 1976 at 4 p.m., from Paris, not London as expected. The itinerary had been modified. The Air France aeroplane had been packed, an endless queue. I waited in the arrival lounge among other people and peered at each passenger emerging from the channel. The passport control was very tight. The police took no chance. I saw several people refused entry and taken away, mainly Asians, from what I could gather. Then Connie appeared, emerging from the jostling crowd. As though I were going to lose her, I literally ran to her, with just a symbolic rose in my hand. I grabbed her and pushed my arm around her. She rested her head on my shoulder as though she were exhausted. She burst into tears. I kept holding her as if she would faint.

'I'm crying because I'm happy,' she said.

That made me cry. 'Who would ever expect you to be here?' I told her.

'Love,' she replied.

I had no response. *God knows how much I love and respect her*, I thought to myself. *Beauty and principle in one single heart.*

I held her hand and took her into a café. The luggage took an age to reach the carousel. We sat on chairs facing each other, holding hands; she looked beautiful, much better than I remembered from Louvain. In good shape, she was wearing jeans, a long cardigan and Nike trainers. Contrast. As though I had just come out of prison, I was thin with long hair, wearing an old jacket from student time, clean but shabby shoes and jeans.

Her luggage arrived. I took care of it, hired a taxi and headed to Mr McGraw's house. We were silent most of the time, but the feeling didn't stop growing. Though she was tired, she was curious, peeking through the window to see a world she had never seen.

Connie didn't ask me to show her Marrakesh or Fes. She was just happy to be with me, and I was equally happy.

25

It was a new dawn. Post-doctoral research had been granted. Before leaving for Southampton, I was advised by Moussa, who was a nationalist and living in Zaio, to see Hjira, an MP, a known figure, nationalist and audacious. He had escaped execution by the French colonialists by mere hours. He hated Jews and despised communists. That was the extent of what I had heard about him.

I went to see him in Rabat. We sat on the terraced café near Hotel Capito, where he stayed and held his surgery. He spoke like a preacher about religion, economics, morality, etc. He was spontaneous, but hard to follow.

'The collapse of the sense of good and bad in man cannot be addressed either by politics or by religion,' he said.

'Circumstances decided I should do some post-doctoral research, but I have no scholarship. Would you like to go with me to see Mr Fassi, an ex-minister, now a representative of UNESCO, to support my application for a scholarship?' I asked.

'UNESCO?' he said. 'UNESCO is full of corrupt elements. It's never clear how a decision is made or who made it. It's an organisation highly corrupt, highly politicised. You stand no chance.'

I went to see Mr Fassi on my own. He looked old, not as sharp as I was expecting him to be. He almost didn't know what I was talking about. I wasted his time and mine with him.

* * *

THE SEVENTH OF JANUARY 1977 WAS a long journey for me. From Rabat to Casablanca, I took a coach, and from Casablanca, I flew to London. By train, I arrived at Southampton late in the afternoon. It was dark and rainy. As I had been advised, I took a taxi to a B&B. I had no idea how big this town was or for what it was famous. From the outside, the B&B looked attractive.

Once in my room, I felt disoriented. The room was small, for single use only, and heated by a small electrical fan. The room was dotted; some areas were hot and others cold.

As Buddha had taught his disciples meditation before action, I sat down, called on my inner energy and mapped my body. England was not Africa. *The sun might not rise or shine, and the rain might persist,* I told myself. *This is a different world, different civilisation, different language and humour. Even love and hate might be expressed differently. We kiss cheeks, shake hands, tap on others' heads. Here, people stand boldly and talk. Maybe this is for hygienic reasons. I must study, listen, learn and adapt for the best or the worst.*

I finished my meditation and went down to the coffee bar. It was open, but my need was food. People twitted and twirled around a girl in the bar behind the counter. *How could one single girl satisfy all those men, even if only emotionally?* I wondered. She looked happy, energetic, and they all looked cheery. *That, in itself, is worth a lot,* I told myself.

I ordered eggs and baked beans. In addition, the landlady brought bacon. It was uncooked. A white fat bordered the two slices.

'I am not a pork eater,' I told her.

She shrugged and picked them off my plate. While drinking a coffee, I was fiddling with some Moroccan bracelets that I had bought on my way to Casablanca. I hadn't had the time to look at them. They were thick, shiny, heavy and pure silver. I bought them in case I became broke. The landlady saw them, became curious and wanted to see them. She touched them and looked impressed.

'For your girlfriend?' she asked. 'Married?'

'Yes,' I answered.

'And how many wives?' she asked.

'Just two,' I said.

'Children?'

'Nine.'

She jumped, went to the bar and told everybody. The entire bar turned to gaze at me, fiddling with my bracelets. If the media were to report real life in north Africa, this lady would know how difficult it is to feed one single person alone, let alone two wives and nine children. Maybe the media reports to entertain, not to inform.

A gay guy, to judge only from the look, came and insisted that I sell him one. He picked the best. I gave it to him free. He was nice and polite.

The morning came, the weather was as dull as the day before and the breakfast was truly British: toast, eggs, mushrooms, bacon and sausages, which I didn't eat. I went to the university to finish my registration. The department was in a modern building and shared with many faculties. The philosophy department was minute compared to Louvain's, which had more than five professors; Southampton had just one. The variety of staff was striking. Manser came from Oxford, David from Oklahoma, Robinson from Harvard and Vallaky was from Czechoslovakia. He had been a monk, met an English woman and ran away with her.

David was my boss. Despite his drama with women, I found him extremely clever. No one in this department was allowed to ignore Wittgenstein. Empiricism was the new Bible. I was told, as primary advice, to discount French methods in thinking and writing, and even in romance, should that happen. It was what one discovered, with no embellishment, that counted.

Heather, the secretary, helped me to find a room in the student accommodation. The room was small, but warm. Six boys were in the flat, and the kitchen was rarely tidy or clean. My neighbour, a French student with no homosexual traits, gave me a shock. It was late, and I was in my bed. He burst in, naked.

'Do you want to have sex with me?' he asked. 'I noticed you have no girlfriend.'

'No, I have a girlfriend,' I answered.

He rushed out in a hurry just as he had rushed in. I had a respectful relationship with him, though he didn't get on with the rest of the boys.

*　　*　　*

TO CONTINUE MY STUDIES, I needed a job, part-time, underpaid, whatever and anywhere. I found a job via an agent in a bakery a few miles away from Southampton. Capitalism was in its ugliest form. No one was allowed to eat the bread or even buy it. It had to be passed to the middle man to put the price that he chose.

While working there, I gave a talk on communism, ultra-socialism. It was difficult to distinguish between communism and Marxism. I argued that communism had failed. It had nothing to offer, and it would, at some stage, collapse. It had had all the time it needed: a generation. If a generation passed, the poverty still persisted and prosperity was elusive, then no borrowing of time should be allowed. The cult of personality was not supposed to be a part of ultra-socialism. When this existed, the system should be counted as failed.

If, in a thousand years, the system were to come back and fulfil its promises – prosperity, no personal cult – the system would then be justified. The system as theory was always correct. Neither the past nor the present could act as a life sentence, either individually or collectively.

I felt vindicated when communism collapsed, and Gorbachev requested help and clothes from the West. Social systems, be they small or big, are like painting, music and dance – a human creation – but the ultimate of all creations is the conscience. In its absence, good and evil are one. Good and evil share the universe, and they alternate as in a revolving door, like the sun and night, summer and winter. But, the conscience is not a product of nature; it is a product of itself.

*　　＊　　＊　　＊*

I RAN COMPLETELY OUT OF money and was not able to pay the rent, the university's fees or my meals, though I never had more than one meal a day. A woman lawyer, academic, and French-educated accepted my request. We went to the bank, spoke to the manager, and I borrowed one hundred pounds.

I advertised to teach French, almost for free, but no one showed an appetite for French learning. The only reply I got was, 'Hi, frog-eater! Come with me; I will teach you to tango.'

I was still looking for a job when a group of well-to-do English people, from different professions, doctors, lawyers, teachers, decided to camp in the south of France, la Bourgogne. They wanted to enjoy the red wine, live among vineyards and test different wines. Not speaking French, they advertised for an interpreter. At first, I hesitated, but then, I applied.

A middle-aged woman interviewed me. She looked like a real bon viveur. She kept me for two hours. She wanted to know everything that I knew about wine, French culture, including dancing and music. During this time, she talked to me like a lover, smiled, showed tenderness, but sometimes she acted like a psychiatrist. I knew she was fishing, wondering if I were a psychopath. As every psychopath had a problem relating to sexuality, she asked some really intimidating questions.

'Are you a virgin?' she asked.

'This question applies only to women,' I answered.

Happy, she gave me the job, and a well-paid one. I was excited: trouble-free, food provided, company, and maybe more.

When I wrote to Connie, she wrote back an almost nasty letter, unhappy that I had to go to France. A week later, she wrote to say that she was coming. Her programme to come, however, never materialised.

At the same time, my passport was with the Home Office. I requested it back, explaining the reason, but the Home Office had more to do than just answer my request. The group, around twenty-eight men and women, single and married, travelled in a luxurious bus. I was left behind to lament my fate.

Suddenly, my landlady received a phone call informing her of the coach's fatal crash on the motorway in the south of France. She ran to my room and couldn't believe her eyes to find me there.

Happening to have escaped death, I focused on finishing my research. Then, I fell ill. It was extreme exhaustion. I couldn't breathe during the night; my heart palpitated with no end. At first, I thought it was acid, but it wasn't. I was advised to stop and rest. I had no choice but to obey.

Connie and I agreed to meet in Scotland, Kilcreggan, at a Christian holiday conference centre. Hamanna, a divorced, mature student, advised me to be on my guard once in Glasgow. She described it as the capital of crime, gangs, sex, etc. I couldn't ignore her kindness.

In Glasgow, however, I saw nothing to match her descriptions. From Glasgow to Kilcreggan, I took a slow train, all alone, and I saw no wealth. Kilcreggan was a spot of paradise. Facing the water, the fresh air invaded my every cell, a healthy spot for a weary body.

Connie arrived a few days later. She knew that I had been extremely exhausted. The spoken words failed to express our joy at seeing each other again. I hugged her as though she were an integral part of myself. She cried a lot, but I couldn't join her in that.

Mornings were conference times. Connie went to every one. There was sailing organised every afternoon, and we didn't miss one single day. Whenever I was late to breakfast, she waited for me, to the extent of missing breakfast twice. That was because I shared a room with a Japanese man. He was a heavy snorer, and with no intervals.

Embarrassed though I was, I kept moving him, but it made no difference. It only got worse. He drove me literally insane. They moved my room, but, unfortunately, they put me with another man who was also a heavy snorer. Whatever discomfort I experienced during the night, the sailing refreshed me.

While in a boat, surrounded by fresh, clean, blue water, the air charging at my face, I asked Connie if she would marry me. She cried and said, 'Yes.'

After a week, Connie left. For the three days I stayed after her departure, as my ticket didn't allow me to travel, I felt utterly lost. I didn't know what to do. It was as though the whole meaning of life had gone away with her. I tried to fill my time with playing volleyball, but it sounded and felt as if I were playing a trick on myself.

* * *

BEFORE I LEFT SOUTHAMPTON FOR Scotland, David, my boss, had bought a big house in a well-to-do quarter. The garage was massive with two doors to accommodate two cars. The previous owner had used the garage as a dump. Evidence of mice and rats filled every corner. For any future use, the garage had to be gutted. To save money, David offered me a job. He didn't expect me to grab it. The offer was cheap, but I was needy. Surprise!

Coming back from Scotland, I couldn't find David, his wife or his children. Unlike Louvain University, or even Frankfurt University, Southampton did not provide a dedicated service to find jobs for its students. The only job in the pipeline was David's offer. I had never known him to lie.

In short: David met a beautiful, young BBC presenter. She won his heart, and he left his wife and family to regenerate himself, as he told me later. Unfortunately, David couldn't keep up with this BBC star. I met him later, a few weeks indeed, and he looked scruffy.

'I am a prey of anxiety,' he told me.

'Middle age?' I asked.

'Middle age tainted with women,' he replied with an ironic smile.

I was not in a much better position than David. Victim of my own imagination, I thought Connie was beginning to slip away from me. Should that happen, I would be emotionally orphaned. I used to receive a letter every day, and her letters balanced the time, brightened my mood and coloured my optimism. Moving from one daily letter to one weekly alarmed me.

Her father, a massive man, had had an operation and absorbed the entire family's time. Connie was the elder daughter. She dedicated her time to shuttling between home and hospital.

Like a cowboy riding in a rodeo, I never knew what was next, up or down. My life was woven with different pieces, each part having its own colour, but I never had an identity problem. Knowing that I was not in the mental hospital sufficed. Strange and bizarre.

I began to understand Jesus Christ. Who was this maverick and enigmatic man? No one seemed to understand. He was surrounded with wells that never dried. Hold a bucket in your hand, with a long and solid rope attached to its end, drop the bucket down, rattle your hand and pull up. The bucket will come full of life's stories, like toads. You can take some home, and there will be enough to pass to your neighbours, friends and enemies alike.

26

Winning over the odds, I finished my study and got my PhD. Nothing, however, was special here except that Fatima and Mohammed, *fille a mama* and *fils a papa* with wealth and power, had been here. Due to their presence, the university had been deemed good. Had they been in Louvain, I would have had no problem.

Now, I was circumcised by the same herd, baptised in the same pond, carried the same flag. As corruption and incompetence fed into each other, would my kite fly high, past the clouds, and be able to pierce the thick, frozen fog?

As I was in a hurry to get a job, I was also in a rush to get married. I ached to leave gypsy life behind, but neither I nor Connie had any money. She might have been richer than me, banking a few dollars in Wells Fargo, but nothing to launch a life *a deux*. It wasn't what I had or what she owned that mysteriously glued us together. We met and differed in many pitches of life.

The date of the wedding was Connie's choice, and with her mother, they took all on board. I was still in Southampton living with Chris and Maggie in an extremely small room and trying to find a publisher. To go ahead with the wedding, identity papers and witnesses from a church were requested. Panic.

Though I went sporadically to an Anglican church with friends, I belonged to no church or denomination. Coming from a Muslim background, surrounded by atheists, sceptics, anti-religious, it was hard to swallow or submit to any dogma. However, thinking no dogma is worth the name of dogma is dogma itself. I was stuck in contradiction.

Taking divorce from my mind, I went to see the minister. He lived in the outskirts of the town in an historic and imposing mansion. As if he were waiting for me, he emerged immediately when I rang the bell.

I had broken the protocol, he told me. I should have first contacted his secretary or at least phoned him before showing up. He taught me an unforgettable lesson.

'Anything to share?' he asked.

'I am getting married and need your signature as a witness,' I said.

He literally went berserk. 'Getting married? To whom?' He probably thought I was kidding him or had escaped from the mental hospital a few miles away.

To confirm my sanity, I mentioned several academic names, including Richard, a member of his congregation. Though I tried to prove my sanity, he gave me the feeling he wasn't sure that I was okay.

To make sure that I got his signature, I went to his parish the following Sunday. It was traditional for the congregation to be offered coffee after the service. I had been in this church before, but it was only now that the minister recognised that I had a face. I could see him doubting, but watching me talk to some members of the congregation made him doubt his own doubt. He came to me with a book in his hand, entitled *Christian Marriage*. I accepted the book and paid the donation.

'Have you signed and posted the request?' I asked him.

'Do it this week,' he responded.

It happened that his preaching that morning had been picked from a novel, *A Man on a Bicycle*. As I wasn't happy that he hadn't signed the paper, and Connie was waiting for it, I took some liberty.

'I came to see you physically, sir. I knocked on your door. I spoke to you, and you still give me the impression that you doubt my intention, yet your entire sermon lacked veracity, was a creation of pure fiction. No man to this day has managed to fly on a bicycle. You paid for the book. You enjoyed the book. You shared its contents with the congregation, yet the entire book is a lie. If the congregation had any mind, they would have left,' I said.

He excused himself and went to speak to somebody else.

*　　*　　*

JUST AS IN A HURRY as I was, Connie fixed the wedding date: the eleventh of April. With speed and efficiency, all preparations were made: the hotel dinner booked, the church building decorated and flowers arranged. Guests, some from far away, were expected, and most of them had already booked their hotel rooms. With just one week left, I was supposed to fly to San Francisco three days before. The ticket was already secured. It was a time of hope.

In this very moment of expectations and dreams, a conscience of identity struck. A crescendo of music pounded in my head, so loud that I had to abort my journey to the library and go back to my room. Looking for comfort, I read Connie's letter. The crescendo of sound got only louder.

Why am I going to marry an American woman? My sisters, with no exception, have all wedded their cousins. All my cousins have either married their cousins or wed within the family. What is safer than marrying one's cousin? Am I a fool? Going out of the net and cutting my blood from its supplies?

Another staccato voice thumped in my heart. *It is not just about the red blood. What about the values, family concepts? Rational and irrational are one. When the rational is analysed, it ends in irrational, and when the irrational is dissected, it ends in rational. Religious deeds and dogma are an opaque mirror. Unlike clothes, they don't go out of fashion.*

I read Connie's letter for a second time. I wanted to decode any hidden meaning that I had missed. Then, my head became a stage. The tenor tried his best, but was only to be contradicted by the bass; the alto took over, but was soon beaten by the soprano. Invaded by the sound of music, I lost the steering wheel. Music with no conductor. *Shall I go to San Francisco? Shall I go? Shall I not? Shall I go? Shall I not?*

I was well aware of the lava in my mind. I was conscious of my psyche being turned into a pitch for rugby players. All that may have been a product of my life's twists – speaking different languages, living in different cultures, being exposed to contradicting religions, not to mention denominations – compounding me with layers of sensitivity. Threshing was a difficult process, and when it came to marrying Connie, all big and small details, be they cultural or religious, carried heavy weight.

27

I had lost Khadija because we had lived in different parts of Morocco. She had been in Fes and I in Kebdana. At least, that was what I believed. Communication was non-existent. Empress with no kingdom, her mother had surveyed and bewitched every member of her family. Letting her blood spill out when there was a chance – Khadija's cousins – would have been an act of betrayal. Acting like a flock of vultures, her family had squeezed any speck of love that she might have harboured for me. Hot-blooded, Moroccan girls could be awkward to drive and cause an earthquake. Had she rebelled, the vultures could have been shooed away.

Khadija's marriage didn't work. She was a divorcee with two children and very little money. She lived on the breadline. I had no pleasure in her pain; I didn't wish her success or ill. I was just indifferent, but with Connie, I was not.

Perpetually déraciné, my life was a conundrum. Going to San Francisco was stepping into the unknown, playing into the hand of Fate. I had little if any knowledge of the country. Contaminated with French and Tarifit, my English accent made me sound like a drug dealer, hence interrogation.

Before I flew to San Francisco, I had requested to stay in a

B&B. Connie booked me a room in El Granada, fifty miles from her parents' home. Though her parents lived in Walnut Creek, California, they were from Arkansas and Illinois.

Connie warned me. 'My parents are from the Midwest, not yet free from prejudice, mental slavery. My aunt still refers to our neighbour as a "nigger" and considered Martin Luther King a trouble-maker and agitator. Besides, my parents are fanatical Christians.'

Connie either hadn't sold me properly or I was unsellable. I flew from Amsterdam and, in the airport, a beautiful, middle-aged woman was roaming around. She was strikingly beautiful, richly clothed, matching her olive skin and dark hair. She spoke to many different people.

'I came from Abu Dhabi,' she told me while we were waiting to depart.

I lost track of her until we landed at San Francisco airport. The woman was taken in a wheelchair, guided to a different direction and gate, accompanied by some armed officers. *Did she get ill while in the sky?* I wondered. *No.* No proof, though.

Entering the United States with a Moroccan passport, coming from England via Amsterdam raised doubt. Politely interrogated, I had to satisfy security questions. Suspicious until proven otherwise, I was told.

A small dog with brown colour, energetically and actively moving, just the size of a fox, sniffed my luggage and my clothes. In a minute, the dog lost interest in me and my belongings and moved, leashed by his master.

'A friend is expecting me outside,' I told two officers – two black women, armed, burly, tough, in no mood to waste their time. No one in his right mind should mess with them. It got tough, and my mind switched back. *If Connie isn't here, I'll take the next flight back.*

Released to enter the land of cowboys, gold and diamonds, I inhaled the damp San Franciscan air. Outside, Connie was waiting, flowers in hand.

She had parked nearby, but my case was heavy to push or pull. She went and came back with her car, an old Honda with new wheels. Serendipitous trip. We drove to El Granada. I stayed in a small, modest, but clean B&B. The dining room was small, tables pushed against each other, and two American couples spoke as loudly as they could. I tried to listen and understand what they were shouting about, but the shouts kept getting louder and louder, and my mind switched off.

It was a week that opened the eyes of the blind. What I saw belied the impression that I carried from a school teacher and an American official. Not everybody lived in a castle, drove a Camaro. As stark as the sunlight, the poverty was visible: infested houses, damp tenements. San Francisco was a pot of gold and silver, but the beggars had their say. Faeces covered the main boulevard. It was a world of diversity, contradiction, tension, competition, elbowing and so on. The biggest sin was the word 'sin'. The flesh was free.

Connie's family was kind and generous. Her father was a war veteran, badly injured. The entire bone of his upper arm had been blown off by a grenade. Two senior surgeons decided to amputate his arm, he told me, but a young surgeon stood in their way.

'Due to him, I didn't lose my arm,' he told me.

'All muscles and no bone, how are you able to use your arm?' I asked.

'The relentless massage and exercise stiffened my muscles. Weak, though, I am using it,' he said.

Connie's dad was a fanatical Christian, and futuristic. Each time around a meal, he brought the problems of time, the Armageddon.

'The world has no more than seven years,' he told everyone at the table.

'What makes you believe that?' I asked him.

He jumped up on his toes, left the table and went to his library. He came back with a Bible in his hand.

'There are omens and prophesies that when China, from the east, starts to build a motorway, this is the ultimate and irrefutable prophesy that time is tidying up.'

'Stop, Daddy, stop!' shouted Connie. 'I'm getting married. I don't care about the time.'

Queen of peace, Connie's mum butted in. 'Your father has always been struggling with the concept of time. Too much reading the Bible.'

Connie's father liked a challenge.

'There is not one single Time. There are many times,' I said.

'How?' he challenged me.

'In an orchestra, there are several musicians; some use violins, some trombones, some French horns, and they are all distinct pieces of time, but altogether, they create one single "Time". But the collapse of one single musician does not stop the melody collectively voiced, albeit there is some change. The conductor's job is to steer and avoid chaos and collision, but yet he is only part of the Time. If there is "Time",' I told him, 'there is also "times". "Times" generate "the Time".'

I found Connie's family interesting. As much as her father was a devout Christian, her sister Martine was a dedicated Unitarian. While Connie's dad was talking at the table, she listened carefully.

With a soft voice, she said, 'I have no problem with my father. He always finds strange things in reading the scripture. I told him once, "You can find anything in the Bible, build anything except an atomic bomb."'

'Which type of religion is Unitarianism?' I asked her.

'It is anything but religion,' she told me with a smile.

'What is your dogma?' I asked her.

'Our dogma is there is no universal dogma. Your conscience is your dogma,' she answered.

Connie and her mother busied themselves with wedding preparations for the next few days: church, dress, flowers, music, and a tuxedo rented for me, her brother and her father.

On the day, having slept in the spare bedroom, I stumbled to the kitchen. Martine was already there, making coffee.

'You can't see Connie today until the wedding, you know. It's bad luck,' she told me.

'Is this a Unitarian concept?' I asked.

'No, it's an old wives' tale,' she said, smiling. 'I'll fix you some coffee and toast, and then you need to get dressed.'

'I'm a little nervous,' I told her.

'Don't worry. The minister will guide you through the service. Just enjoy it and know that you're getting a very good wife,' she said.

'I know. I'll try to take good care of her,' I said.

I sat down, had my coffee and toast in silence, then scuttled off to get dressed. The tuxedo fit fairly well, but I couldn't tie the bowtie. Returning to the kitchen, I again found Martine.

'You look incredible!' she remarked. 'But Connie needs to fatten you a little. She's a very good cook.'

'I'm looking forward to that. Do you know how to tie this bowtie?' I asked.

'Sure, come here. And I have your boutonniere.'

Complete, I went to look at myself. I didn't recognise myself in the mirror. Noting the tails, I thought, *I could be a monkey.*

'Jusef!' called Connie's father. 'It's time to go to the church!'

The church was larger than I had imagined, and grander, with a huge spire reaching to God. As I walked inside, a rush of cool air and a peaceful calm enveloped me. I could see there were already some people seated. The minister greeted us and ushered me to the front of the church through a side door. Connie's brother, Max, already seated, was my best man, even though I hardly knew him.

'You two sit here and stand up when I give the cue,' the minister told us. 'Jusef, I'll direct you as we go along. Don't worry about a thing.'

He doesn't know how foreign I feel here, but this is a new beginning with Connie and with God, I thought to myself.

After ten minutes of fidgeting, I was motioned to stand and face the aisle. The music played louder, and Connie, accompanied by her father, was walking slowly down the aisle toward me.

I've never seen her look like this! She's so decorated. Beautiful! I thought. *And she's all mine!* She reached the end of the aisle, and we stood facing each other. From that point on, my mind was in a haze. I performed as instructed, but I could see only her, and then it was over. I kissed her with a rush of bravado and desire I didn't know I had.

As we walked back down the aisle and out of the church, people bombarded us with confetti and rice. It was as if I were beginning my life anew.

REVIEWS OF *A RIFFIAN'S TUNE*

'A magnificent read. Each page will hold you in its clutches and squeeze from you so much emotion and the need to keep turning the pages. Moroccan culture is seen from the inside, both the positive and the negative. The story overflows with tragedies, courage and triumphs. Jusef shows the reader the power of hope and the strength to believe in a positive future. I absolutely loved this book and wished it had carried on further. It is a wonderful book.'

'Joseph Labaki's writing reminded me of a cross between Hemmingway and Paulo Coelho, having the same simple but elegant style, and the succinct clarity which is so effective in transporting the reader to places and times they would never otherwise see. I thoroughly enjoyed *A Riffian's Tune*. It made me laugh, cry and think and above all is a beautiful book.'

'You HAVE to read this book!'

'A riveting read – to discover the things Jusef went through makes you feel so humbled; each obstacle in his life makes you want him to succeed even more. You simply can't put the book down! Beautifully written; the descriptions pull you firmly to each time and place in a world far away. It is a truly heart-wrenching read.'

Publishers Weekly

'The autobiographical novel of a Moroccan boy's solo climb from the grip of poverty, ignorance, tradition, superstition and religion; rich with culture, humor and deeply moving stories.'